ON THE EGO & THE LOVE OF PRAISE

POPE SHENOUDA III

On the Ego & the Love of Praise
By Pope Shenouda III

Copyright © 2025 Coptic Orthodox Diocese of the Southern U.S.A.

All rights reserved.

Designed & Published by:
St. Mary & St. Moses Abbey Press
101 S Vista Dr, Sandia, TX 78383
stmabbeypress.com

All Scripture quotations in the footnotes of this book, unless otherwise indicated, are taken from the New King James Version® Copyright © 1982 by Thomas Nelson, Inc. Used by permission. All rights reserved.

Cover illustration by Ann Mary Ibrahim.

Contents

PART ONE: ON THE EGO   5

  Introduction   6

  1. On the Self (Ego)   8

  2. Love of Self: A Mother Sin   16

  3. Reasons Behind a Heightened Sense of Self and the Sins that Follow it?   24

  4. The Ego is the Cause of Many Other Sins   41

  5. He who Loves His Life will Lose It   51

  6. How to Eliminate the Self (the Ego)   65

  7. "Not I"   80

PART TWO: ON THE LOVE OF PRAISE   92

  1. Degrees of Sin in the Love of Praise   93

  2. Evils that Result from the Love of Praise   99

  3. How does a Person Flee from the Love of Praise and Honor   106

PART ONE

ON THE EGO

Introduction

The ego is one of the principal spiritual wars.[1] In fact, it is perhaps the most important thing that hinders the spiritual life and breaks it down. The ego was the reason behind the fall of a great angel of the rank of the cherubim, so he became the Devil and a leader of demons, when he said in his heart, "I will ascend into heaven, I will exalt my throne above the stars of God;... I will be like the Most High."[2]

The love of self is a mother sin that gives birth to a multitude of sins. Of it, pride is born, and jealousy, and also envy, and of it, much strife is born between people, even between siblings. The lover of his self falls into the sin of selfishness and favors himself above all. And he loves taking constantly rather than giving, and loves the praise of people and even pursues it. The ego may also lead to boastfulness and haughtiness.

---

1   Or: the self. We use both words throughout the translation as best suits the context. The Arabic text uses two words: one is *al-that* that is "the self," and the other *al-ana* that is literally "the I" or the ego.
2   Isaiah 14:13–14.

Perhaps the reason for falling into many lusts may be a desire to satisfy the self, but in the wrong way.

This book in your hands will speak about all of this and about numerous other sins that the ego causes. We will also speak about the reasons behind the heightened sense of self, and about the methods God sometimes employs to cure His children of the ego, or to protect them from it. Contained within this book is also a chapter on how to eliminate the ego. This is done by putting in place spiritual means for this purpose, and exercises by which the spiritual person can progress to self-denial, to self-condemnation sometimes, and to the phrase "No longer I, but…"

How beautiful is the saying of the Lord Jesus Christ, glory be to Him: "He who loves his life will lose it."[3]

Pope Shenouda III

---

[3] John 12:25.

Chapter 1
On the Self (Ego)

The Ego was the First Sin the World Knew

Satan fell in it before man did. The devil, the "cherub who covers,"[4] "full of wisdom and perfect in beauty,"[5] fell when he said in his heart, "I will ascend into heaven, I will exalt my throne above the stars of God;… I will ascend above the heights of the clouds, I will be like the Most High."[6] This love of self cast him down into the lowest depths of Hades, and so it [the self] descended instead of ascending!

As the Devil fell through the ego, so did man, too. When God created him, man knew that his self was derived from God, for God is the one who brought it into being, who granted it all gifts and talents. And it cannot live without Him. Through God alone, he used to obtain all the knowledge he needed. Then man fell when his self departed from God.

---
4   Ezekiel 28:14.
5   Ezekiel 28:12.
6   Isaiah 14:13–14.

Part One: On the Ego

For they took counsel from a source other than God, and even submitted to the serpent's enticement that "your eyes will be opened, and you will be like God, knowing good and evil."[7] And so, the self departed from God, through disobedience on the one hand, and through its desire to be like God on the other hand, in the same way as that of the Devil who said, "I will be like the Most High."

The worst thing a person can fall into is loving his self with a wrong love; therefore, they wish to magnify themselves in their own eyes, or to become righteous in their own eyes.

No person hates himself. Even when God commanded concerning the love of neighbor, He said, "You shall love your neighbor as yourself."[8] The true love of self is to make it cling to God. As the psalmist said, "But as for me, it is good to cling to God."[9] In its love for God, it will love its neighbor also, and this love will reach the point of self-sacrifice for the sake of God as well as the neighbor.

As for the wrong love, it is a sort of selfishness, in which the ego (self) leads to egotism (selfishness). And so a man becomes centered around his self and all that is related to it: his dignity, his position, his money, his outdoing of others, even his control over them. His ego wants to climb up, even if [that is] upon the skulls

---

7 Genesis 3:5.

8 Matthew 22:39.

9 Psalms 72:28 LXX, Orthodox Study Bible.

of others. He wants to rest, even if at the expense of others' toil. He builds his self, even if at the cost of the destruction of others!

In the love of self, man wants to receive and not give. If he gave, it would be so that he may receive, receiving praise and esteem, or receiving a compensation he desires. It is a state of a person who is always preoccupied with his self, giving it that which satisfies it both psychologically and materially. He constantly favors it over all, and has no objection to clashing with everyone whom he sees as a rival for this self or as an obstacle in its way.

Many have fallen into the love of self and of satisfying it, so it ruined them, or came close to doing so.

Examples from the Old and New Testaments

An example of this is Solomon, who fulfilled the desires of the self. Yes, Solomon the wise, who was the wisest man of the people of the earth in his time, became preoccupied with his self and his pleasures. Therefore, he said:

> I made my works great, I built myself houses, and planted myself vineyards. I made myself gardens and orchards.... I made myself water pools from which to water the growing trees of the grove.... I also gathered for myself silver and gold and the special treasures of kings and of the provinces. I acquired male and female singers, the delights of

the sons of men, and musical instruments of all kinds. So I became great and excelled more than all who were before me in Jerusalem. Also my wisdom remained with me. Whatever my eyes desired I did not keep from them.[10]

And what was the result? The desires of this self almost ruined Solomon. And so was the result, which is the saying of the Scripture about him:

For it was so, when Solomon was old, that his wives turned his heart after other gods; and his heart was not loyal to the LORD his God, as was the heart of his father David. For Solomon went after Ashtoreth the goddess of the Sidonians, and after Milcom the abomination of the Ammonites. Solomon did evil in the sight of the LORD.[11]

Thus, he deserved that the Lord punish him.[12] As Solomon was, who was preoccupied with his self, so was Jonah also. God sent him to preach to Nineveh, but he feared that they would heed the warning coming from his mouth and repent, and then the word of Jonah would be made void when God relented of His fierce anger against Nineveh! And so, seeking to preserve his dignity and the repute of his words, he first fled from God, taking a ship

---

10 Ecclesiastes 2:4–10.

11 1 Kings 11:4–6.

12 See 1 Kings 11:9–11.

to Tarshish. When God brought him back with a miracle, and he preached to Nineveh, and so they repented and God had mercy on them, Jonah was angry and said, "It is better for me to die than to live!"[13]

Thus, in his love for his self and the esteem of his word, he preferred that 120,000 souls should perish rather than that his word fall, being angry at the mercies of God who relented from His fierce anger and accepted the Ninevites' repentance.[14]

Another example of the ego, which has caused some to perish, was King Ahab's desire to possess Naboth the Jezreelite's vineyard.[15] He was not satisfied with all that he had as a king, but desired Naboth's vineyard [too]. His wife, Queen Jezebel, assisted him in fulfilling the desire of the self, and so she arranged for false witnesses to testify that Naboth the Jezreelite had blasphemed against God and the king. The matter culminated in his stoning and death, and Ahab fulfilled his self's desire: taking possession of Naboth's vineyard.

But did Ahab truly please his self with what he did and what he took possession of? No. Rather, God's punishment came to him by the mouth of the prophet Elijah, saying to him, "In the place where dogs licked the blood of Naboth, dogs shall lick your blood, even yours."[16]

---

13 Jonah 4:3.
14 See Jonah 3:9–10.
15 See 1 Kings 21.
16 1 Kings 21:19.

We must treat the effects of the war of the ego from childhood, when a child says "I" and wants to own everything he can get his hands on. [From the time when] he becomes jealous of his siblings and wants to take away what is given to them, and even gets jealous of every word of praise directed at them and from all the love they receive, supposing that both the praise and the love are his right alone. For this reason, we must train the child to love and to give, from an early age, and give them things to give to others, and encourage them to give.

The ego warred against Christ's holy disciples and apostles themselves when they were disputing among themselves about who would be the greatest among them. The Lord rebuked them, saying, "You know that those who are considered rulers over the Gentiles lord it over them, and their great ones exercise authority over them. Yet it shall not be so among you; but whoever desires to become great among you shall be your servant. And whoever of you desires to be first shall be slave of all."[17]

How marvelous it is that the greatest among those born of women, that is, John the Baptist,[18] was the person who was most able to dispose of the ego in his relationship with Christ. When the Lord approached him to be baptized, he said to Him, "I need to be baptized by You."[19] When he saw the masses following the Master,

---

17 Mark 10:42–44.

18 See Matthew 11.

19 Matthew 3:14.

he said, "He who has the bride is the bridegroom; but the friend of the bridegroom, who stands and hears him, rejoices greatly.... He must increase, but I must decrease. He who comes from above is above all."[20]

The Cure for the Ego

Self-denial is truly the greatest cure for the ego. Your self is what wars against you more than Satan does. [In fact,] when Satan wars against you, he first wars against you through this ego [or self].

If you triumph over your self, you will, undoubtedly, triumph over the rest of the sins. For you are your own greatest enemy. No human would be able to offend you[21] if you were victorious over your self[22] within yourself. As St. John Chrysostom said, "Do you then perceive that if a man does not injure himself, no one else will be able to harm him?"[23]

Try, then, to acquire divine power by not relying on yourself. As the Scripture says, "Do not be wise in your own eyes; fear the LORD and depart from evil."[24] Try to acquire humility through self-denial and by not being righteous in your own eyes.

---

20 John 3:29–31.

21 Literally: make you stumble.

22 Or: ego.

23 St. John Chrysostom, *No One can Harm the Man who does not Injure Himself,* Stephens W.R.W., trans. (Sandia, TX: St. Mary and St. Moses Abbey Press, 2025), 49.

24 Proverbs 3:7.

For what was the righteous Job's problem, except this? He was a righteous man and knew that he was righteous, and so he was righteous in his own eyes. Because of this, he was unable to bear his three friends' words, and he said to them, "I am blameless, yet I do not know myself,"[25] and said to the Lord, "I am afraid of all my sufferings; I know that You will not hold me innocent. If I am condemned, why then do I labor in vain? If I wash myself with snow water, and cleanse my hands with soap, yet You will plunge me into the pit, and my own clothes will abhor me."[26] His argument with his friends ended with the saying of the Scripture: "So these three men ceased answering Job, because he was righteous in his own eyes."[27]

Job's trial did not end except after he rejected this self and its righteousness, saying to the Lord, "I have uttered what I did not understand, things too wonderful for me, which I did not know.... Therefore I abhor myself, and repent in dust and ashes."[28] When Job's self [or ego] reached the dust and ashes, then his trial ended, "and the LORD restored Job's losses."[29]

All that remains for me to say to you is that the self is a fertile mother, begetting many sins.

---

25 Job 9:21.
26 Job 9:28–31.
27 Job 32:1.
28 Job 42:3, 6.
29 Job 42:10.

Chapter 2

Love of Self: A Mother Sin

We say that it is one of the mother sins because the love of self—that is, the wrong love of self—is a fertile mother, begetting a multitude of sins.

One of the first sins that the ego begets is pride. The one who cares for the ego constantly wants to inflate his self such that it becomes great in his eyes and in the eyes of others, and in this he becomes infatuated with himself. And he may fall into what is called "narcissism." His self is very beautiful in his own eyes, like those who love to constantly look in the mirror and contemplate their beautiful features.

From here, one who falls into the love of the ego might also fall into conceit. He may think more highly of himself than he really is; he feels that his self is valuable. He thinks that he is something, that he has special importance or special talents, or that he is better than others: He understands more or has a greater position.

This feeling gives him excessive self-confidence; he wants to impose it on others. Through this feeling, he is led to grandeur and the love of first places.

This sense of self may come to a person in their adolescence, when they feel that they have moved on to a higher stage that grants them a particular importance. Too often, this juvenile feeling persists throughout the course of their lives, taking on different forms, however, than those of adolescence.

This feeling may also occur to a child because of excessive praise or encouragement, or excellence [at something], or special abilities. While this feeling may not be dangerous in a child, it usually deviates in adults.

In all this, the self-absorbed person is as distant as one can possibly be from humility. This is because his love for honor may stand in the way of attaining a life of humility. For he views humility as an undermining of his significance, and as something that separates him from the greatness which he desires for himself. He loves for his self to be respected by all, and he even relishes that he be the only one respected. He wants to be the sole object of people's interest and appreciation.

Because of this, he might even fall into the sins of jealousy and envy. In this jealousy, he wants to get everything for himself: praise, money, admiration, success, excellence, attention. Not only does he love that his self be praised, but he wants all praise to be for him alone. If another is praised, his self becomes troubled and distressed, as if this other person who was praised robbed him of a right due only to him.

And so the self or the ego was the cause of the struggles that the Scripture has recorded. Because of the ego, Cain rose against his brother Abel and killed him, because Abel was more righteous than him, and [because] God had acknowledged Abel and accepted his sacrifice.[30]

Because of the ego, a dispute arose between Abram and Lot, and the Scripture said about them, "Now the land was not able to support them, that they might dwell together.... And there was strife between the herdsmen of Abram's livestock and the herdsmen of Lot's livestock."[31] For whom shall the grassy land be? Even our holy father Abram said to his nephew Lot, "Please let there be no strife between you and me, and between my herdsmen and your herdsmen; for we are brethren. Is not the whole land before you? Please separate from me. If you take the left, then I will go to the right; or, if you go to the right, then I will go to the left."[32] And thus they parted ways.

Also, because of the ego, enmity arose between Jacob and Esau, who were brothers. Jacob said in his heart, "I will take the birthright instead of my brother," and he took advantage of his brother's hunger and fatigue, and purchased the birthright from him for

---

30 See Genesis 4.
31 Genesis 13:6–7.
32 Genesis 13:8–9.

a meal of lentils.[33] With the same ego, he returned and plotted, with his mother's assistance, to take for himself the blessing instead of his brother, having no qualms, to achieve this, about deceiving his weak-sighted father and lying, and saying to his father, "I am Esau your firstborn."[34] Esau also, to avenge himself, said in his heart, "The days of mourning for my father are at hand; then I will kill my brother Jacob."[35]

The ego also brought about a struggle between two sisters: Leah and Rachel. Each one wanted to win the man and to compete with her sister to have more children, such that, in this struggle for the love of their shared husband and in this competition over bearing children, Rachel said, "With great wrestlings I have wrestled with my sister, and indeed I have prevailed."[36] In this struggle, each one gave her maid to Jacob so that he might beget offspring from them, which would be counted for them.

Because of the ego, also, Peninnah used to annoy Hannah. For Peninnah had children, but her husband's other wife, Hannah, was barren, Peninnah continued to upset her until she made her weep, and she could not eat out of her intense resentment and sorrow.[37] It is as if Peninnah was saying, "I am the one with children; she has none."

---

33 See Genesis 25:29–34.
34 Genesis 27:19.
35 Genesis 27:41.
36 Genesis 30:8.
37 See 1 Samuel 1:2–7.

With the same ego, Martha complained about her sister Mary, who sat at Jesus' feet, her feeling being: "Why do I toil while Mary rests, listening to the Lord?" And so did she say to Him, "Lord, do You not care that my sister has left me to serve alone? Therefore tell her to help me."[38]

With the same ego, King Saul was hostile toward David and sought to kill him. He was irritated by him, became jealous of him, and envied him because the women praised David more than him (when he killed Goliath) and sang, saying, "Saul has slain his thousands, and David his ten thousands."[39] "Then Saul was very angry, and the saying displeased him; and he said, 'They have ascribed to David ten thousands, and to me they have ascribed only thousands. Now what more can he have but the kingdom?'"[40] From then on, he expended all his effort to kill David who had saved him and saved the entire army from the mighty Goliath. Such, however, is the self!

Because of the self, the older brother was displeased with the honor which his father gave to his repentant brother. For when he heard the sound of joy at the return of his brother, he was angry and did not want to enter the house, nor to participate in the joy for his brother's return. When his father came out to him to invite him inside, he reproached him firmly, focusing on his self, by saying to his father:

---

38 Luke 10:40.
39 1 Samuel 18:7.
40 1 Samuel 18:8.

> Lo, these many years I have been serving you; I never transgressed your commandment at any time; and yet you never gave me a young goat, that I might make merry with my friends. But as soon as this son of yours came, who has devoured your livelihood with harlots, you killed the fatted calf for him.[41]

Truly, focusing on one's self may destroy the love between siblings and kindred. It may even bring about enmity between them, enmity that may develop into murder, or at the very least, the matter might culminate in a competition and struggle, or in complaints and criticism. For the same reason, relatives part ways, like what happened with Abram and Lot.

Likewise, we notice that one who cares about the ego concentrates on self-fulfillment. He does not think about the kingdom of God, but rather about his own kingdom. The kingdom of God does not preoccupy him, but rather he is preoccupied with his self and how to fulfill its existence and ambitions. Even in his prayer, he sees that God's primary work is to give his self a presence and to magnify his self for him, on earth and in heaven. And his prayers consist of nothing but the phrases, "I want... and I want!"

The one who focuses on his ego wants everyone to fulfill it for him. The society around him has to fulfill his ego for him. The Church's duty is to fulfill his ego

---

41 Luke 15:29–30.

for him. Likewise, this is the function of the father of confession. If he joins a service, his objective is that it too may fulfill his ego for him!

And if this does not take place, he revolts against everyone! He revolts against the Church if he finds that she does not fulfill his ego for him. He revolts against the father of confession if he sees that he does not fulfill his ego for him. And he distances himself from the religious sphere altogether, indignant against it, because he does not find his ego in it. Not only that, but every single person who does not fulfill his ego for him, he distances himself from them, even from God Himself!

This perhaps reminds us of the existentialists and atheists, each of whom searches for their own existence, and how to enjoy this existence, and as though their state of being says: "It is better that God is not, so that I am!" The meaning of existence with them is to enjoy pleasures, and in their view, pleasure is linked to matter and the senses. If God's commandment stands in opposition to their bodily and material enjoyment, then neither God nor His commandment exists! To such an extent do the ego and self lead.

All the joy of the lovers of self is in receiving, not in giving. They believe that, by receiving, they build up the self and enlarge it, and add new things to it. They remind us of the rich fool who said, "I will pull down my barns and build greater, and there I will store all my crops and my goods. And I will say to my soul,

'Soul, you have many goods laid up for many years; take your ease; eat, drink, and be merry.'"[42]

As for giving, it is observed by the person who forsakes caring about his self, to care about others, who believes that "it is more blessed to give than to receive."[43]

---

[42] Luke 12:18–19.
[43] Acts 20:35.

Chapter 3

Reasons Behind a Heightened Sense of Self and the Sins that Follow it?

What are the Reasons Behind a Heightened Sense of Self?

There are many reasons for a person to be fought with the self. One reason is the talents, like the arts in their various forms. This is especially true for those who have reached a high level in this affair. An example of this is an ingenious artist in Italy, to whom one of his admirers sent a letter. They did not write the name of the artist on the envelope, but were satisfied with the phrase "To the greatest artist in Italy." They delivered the letter to this artist, but he did not accept it, saying, "It is not for me. If its sender intended me, they would have written, 'To the greatest artist in the world!'" These are the talents that some use not only to feel the [sense of] self and its greatness, but through these talents, they might also become conceited.

Of course, we do not say that all those endowed with talents are fought with a heightened sense of self, for how beautiful it is when some join talents and humility together. An example of this is St. Paul the Apostle, who had a great many talents. Nevertheless, he used to say, "By the grace of God I am what I am;... yet not I, but the grace of God which was with me."[44] Likewise, let us remember the saints who had supernatural gifts, like raising the dead or performing other miracles, and [yet] they did not lose their humility. None of them said the word "I."

In addition to talents, in being fought with the self, are the rest of the abilities. For example, if someone has an ability in something that others do not, or if they reach the level of champion in some sport, or if they become geniuses in a particular science, they reach, in all this, a spectacular level. And this excellence and this ability may be a reason for a heightened sense of self.

A heightened sense of self can also be caused by lineage, wealth, or position, like a person of a distinguished lineage, from a noble family that has a glorious history. He would boast about this lineage and would feel that he was superior to others in this.

In the same way, a person may have a heightened sense of self through wealth if they reach a degree that allows them to be prominent in society, to do whatever they please with money, and to gain friends, followers, and disciples with it.

---

44 1 Corinthians 15:10.

A person may also have a heightened sense of self through their position, if it is a lofty position and brings them authority, respect, and influence. Their sense of the loftiness of their position may cause them to have a heightened sense of self, a self that can give orders, and others obey.

A person may have a heightened sense of self because of their intelligence and success. A person's sense of self heightens if he understands what others do not, and can deduce what others cannot, and can find solutions to problems others are powerless before, and is observant and quick-witted while others stand perplexed, oblivious to what is going on—and so in all this he feels as if he were on a much higher level than others.

Success also gives one a heightened sense of self, especially if the success is continual: "Whatever he does shall prosper."[45] Of course, not all people are like this, for Joseph the righteous was prosperous in all things[46] and was not fought with the self; rather, it was God who made him prosperous in all that he did.

Likewise, another possible reason for a heightened sense of self may be a man's power or a woman's beauty. David felt his power when he threatened Nabal the Carmelite, that he would not leave one male [alive] of all who belonged to Nabal by morning light.[47] Thus,

---

45 Psalms 1:3.
46 See Genesis 39.
47 See 1 Samuel 25.

we see that a sense of self heightened by power may sometimes lead to revenge. Also, Samson the mighty: did he not have a heightened sense of self because of his strength? And likewise, Delilah: did she not have a heightened sense of self because of her beauty, which enabled her to control this mighty man and seduce him into divulging the secret of his strength?

A person can also have a heightened sense of self because of people's praise of him. King Herod fell into this trap when the sycophantic crowd said to him, "'The voice of a god and not of a man!' Then immediately an angel of the Lord struck him, because he did not give glory to God. And he was eaten by worms and died."[48] People's constant praise may perhaps make one feel that he[49] is infallible, that he is above the level of falling into error. He is always "righteous in his own eyes"[50] and wise in his own eyes, and this is one of the maladies of the heightened sense of self.

To avoid this heightened sense of self, God permitted weaknesses to some of the saints. Thus, we see the great saint Paul the Apostle, who was worthy of being taken up to the third heaven, into Paradise, and of hearing inexpressible words not lawful for a man to utter,[51] say, "And lest I should be exalted above measure by the abundance of the revelations, a thorn in the flesh was given to me, a messenger of Satan to

---

48   Acts 12:22–23.
49   Literally: his self.
50   Job 32:1.
51   See 2 Corinthians 12:4.

buffet me, lest I be exalted above measure."[52] And this thorn remained with him, despite his pleading three times that it might depart from him.

And because he was met with much glory from people, we find him say, to counterbalance the self, "By honor and dishonor, by evil report and good report."[53] And so this great saint entered the trial of dishonor and evil report, so that he may not sense his self in his ministry, both he and his companions in the ministry.

Another example, besides St. Paul the Apostle, is the patriarch Jacob. He received the blessing and the birthright and was told, "Be master over your brethren, and let your mother's sons bow down to you."[54] He received the blessing from his father, Isaac, and [received] the blessing and promises from God Himself,[55] and wrestled with God and men and prevailed,[56] and received a new name from God.[57] Nevertheless, there had to be a balance so that he would not fall into a heightened sense of self.

Therefore, God permitted that Jacob remain afraid and terrified of his brother Esau; and permitted his uncle Laban to trick him more than once; and even [permitted] that his sons trick him by telling him that Joseph had been killed by a wild beast; and

---

52 2 Corinthians 12:7.
53 2 Corinthians 6:8.
54 Genesis 27:29.
55 See Genesis 28.
56 See Genesis 32:28.
57 Ibid.

[permitted] that his sons cause him a problem with the peoples of the land by killing Shechem and his people; and permitted many hardships to [befall] him, such that he said to Pharaoh, "Few and evil have been the days of the years of my life."[58] And when the Lord blessed him, and he struggled with God and men and prevailed, God struck him in his hip socket, and he limped because of it all his days so that he might sense his weakness and not be haughty.

With the same balance, God treated Abraham, the patriarch and the father of the prophets. For despite being one of the greatest men of faith (since by faith he went to offer his son as a sacrifice to God,[59] and in his obedience to God also, he left his country, his family, and his father's house and departed, not knowing where he was going[60]), and despite him receiving magnificent promises from God, who said to him, "I will bless you;… you shall be a blessing. I will bless those who bless you;… and in you all the families of the earth shall be blessed,"[61] God left a weakness with Abraham—that is, fear.

And so, he feared when he went down to Egypt, and said that Sarah was his sister, so that they would not kill him because of her. He had the same fear when he went down to Gerar, and also said that Sarah was his sister, so King Abimelech took her, but God rescued

---

58 Genesis 47:9.
59 See Genesis 22.
60 See Genesis 12.
61 Genesis 12:2–3.

her from him. This fear was beneficial for our father Abraham, so that he might not have a heightened sense of self, he who had been victorious in the war of the kings, and had rescued Lot and those who were taken captive from Sodom.[62]

The same also applies to St. Peter the Apostle, whom the Lord called blessed when he said, "You are the Christ, the Son of the living God."[63] Peter, of whom the sense of self took hold to such an extent that he felt he had a stronger love for and loyalty to the Lord than all the disciples, said to Him, "Even if all are made to stumble because of You, I will never be made to stumble,"[64] and "Lord, I am ready to go with You, both to prison and to death."[65]

For this Peter, God permitted the trial in which he denied Him three times, and so "he went out and wept bitterly."[66] After the Resurrection, the Lord also brought him outside the circle of the sense of self, and he called him by his secular name three times, saying to him, "Simon, son of Jonah, do you love Me more than these?... Peter was grieved because He said to him the third time, 'Do you love Me?'"[67] As for the phrase "more than these," it was [said] to remind him of his words, "If all are made to stumble because of

---

62 See Genesis 14.
63 Matthew 16:16.
64 Matthew 26:33. Also see Mark 14:29.
65 Luke 22:33.
66 Matthew 26:75.
67 John 21:15, 17.

You, I will never be made to stumble." Peter's denial continued to prick his heart every time the enemy fought him with the ego and sense of self, so much so that at the hour of his crucifixion, he asked to be crucified upside down.

This balance between the sense of self and the duties of humility, God also established in the life of Solomon the wise: Solomon, whom God Himself chose to build His temple, and to whom He appeared twice, once in Gibeon and again in Jerusalem, and whom He granted wisdom from above such that there were none like him in his wisdom upon the whole earth, so that the queen of Sheba came from the ends of the earth to hear Solomon's wisdom, and he also whom the Lord granted royal majesty the likes of which no one else had.[68]

This Solomon, who obtained wealth and worldly pleasure that no other king had ever had, who said, "So I became great and excelled more than all who were before me in Jerusalem,"[69] who made for himself "gardens and orchards,"[70] who "acquired male and female singers, the delights of the sons of men, and musical instruments of all kinds,"[71] and who said in all this, "Whatever my eyes desired I did not keep from them"[72]—God permitted a weak point for this

---

68 See 1 Kings 3–8.
69 Ecclesiastes 2:9.
70 Ecclesiastes 2:5.
71 Ecclesiastes 2:8.
72 Ecclesiastes 2:10.

great Solomon, which was his love for women and his submission to their influence, so it made him lose his wisdom and perfection.

This permission was through grace's abandonment of him a little because of his indulgence in the pleasures of the flesh, for so it was said about him, "For it was so, when Solomon was old, that his wives turned his heart after other gods; and his heart was not loyal to the LORD his God, as was the heart of his father David."[73] And Solomon deserved punishment from God, but he benefited from God's disciplining of him and repented.

Let every person fear the heightened sense of self, and let them remember the Lord's saying, "If anyone desires to come after Me, let him deny himself."[74]

The Multitude of Sins that are Born of the Self

Man's first and biggest problem—if not his only—is the self. For if we put on display the sins that come forth from the self, we would find that they are nearly all the sins.

For this reason, a person who is internally victorious over his self is a victorious person all-around, and the person who is defeated by his self might be defeated by anything. Hence, how beautiful is St. John Chrysostom's saying, "Do you then perceive

---

73 1 Kings 11:4.
74 Matthew 16:24.

that if a man does not injure himself, no one else will be able to harm him?"[75] That is, if a person does not harm himself, no one will be able to harm him. For spiritual harm does not come to one from the outside as much as it comes from the inside, from his self.

Abba Isaac [the Syrian] spoke the truth, saying, "Be peaceful within yourself, and heaven and earth will be at peace with you."[76] And the expression "be peaceful within yourself" means that the person should not be the adversary of the self, distancing it from God and from good.

One of the famous sins is the attempt to magnify the self. Self-magnification comes in two types: either magnifying it in and of itself, or magnifying it by way of comparison, by comparing it to others, so it would be bigger than others, better, stronger, greater, more beautiful, and more intelligent.

The devil fell into both matters together. Concerning magnifying his self in and of itself, he said, "I will ascend into heaven.... I will ascend above the heights of the clouds,"[77] and concerning the comparison, he said, "I will exalt my throne above the stars of God.... I will be like the Most High."[78]

---

75 St. John Chrysostom, *No One can Harm the Man who does not Injure Himself,* Stephens W.R.W., trans. (Sandia, TX: St. Mary and St. Moses Abbey Press, 2025), 49.
76 *The Ascetical Homilies of Saint Isaac the Syrian.* (Boston, MA: Holy Transfiguration Monastery, 2011), 121.
77 Isaiah 14:13–14.
78 Ibid.

With the same approach, the devil fought the first human: with magnification of the self, by saying to Adam and Eve, "You will be like God, knowing good and evil."[79] Man also fell through the pleasure which he wanted to provide for his self, for he "saw that the tree was good for food, that it was pleasant to the eyes, and a tree desirable."[80]

Therefore, one of the sins that the self is fought with is pleasure. Pleasure wars against the flesh and the senses through lust. On this, St. John the Apostle said, "The lust of the flesh, the lust of the eyes, and the pride of life.... And the world is passing away, and the lust of it."[81] And here, to the lusts of the flesh which the self takes pleasure in, he added the lust of the soul, that is, the pride of life. The person who loves his self seeks to grant it pleasure through all its forms: by sense, touch, sight, food and drink, and the pleasures of the flesh.

He is constantly self-centered. His self is everything in his sight. His desires come first, and his interests first, and his opinions first. He so cares for his self that he does not care about anyone [else], and to obtain what he desires, he may clash with others or mistreat them. He has no objection to opposing everyone in order to accomplish what his self wants. His focus on his self blinds him to everything!

---

[79] Genesis 3:5.
[80] Genesis 3:6.
[81] 1 John 2:16–17.

And in his love of self, he may abundantly praise his self, and glorify it. He speaks about himself, but his speech is neither complete nor fair. For he talks about nothing but its virtues, glories, and victories, and conceals its flaws. If someone exposes some of these flaws, he tries to justify the self and defend it.

This person, who praises himself, is often very sensitive. He is, for instance, sensitive regarding his dignity and rights. The smallest thing upsets or hurts him. The slightest advice, reproof, or blame hurts his feelings, and he cannot endure it. And he, too often, feels unjustly treated or cheated out of his rights, and feels that people do not give him sufficient attention or the appropriate respect. For this reason, he complains on many occasions and grumbles because his ego does not receive the space he wants for it. And for this reason, he is easy to clash with and have friction with.

He may resort to withdrawing into his self, contemplating its beauties by himself, without being wounded by others, fleeing from this society that does not grant him what is rightfully his and that does not fulfill his self for him. Conversely, he might interfere in everything, thinking that by this he is giving his self a chance to be seen!

He loves himself with an unwise and unsound love. The Lord's saying applies to him, "He who finds his life will lose it."[82] For while he desires to build himself

---

82 Matthew 10:39.

up, we see him demolish it, and while he desires to magnify it, he destroys it. In all this, he desires to build himself up from outside with a false appearance, while the psalm says, "All the glory of the daughter of the King is within."[83]

In his heightened sense of self and excessive confidence in it, he always relies on himself. In all the problems or difficulties that he encounters, he solely relies on his human arm, his effort, his intelligence, his own abilities, and his good behavior. Meanwhile, the spiritual person relies on the grace that comes to him from above, on the work of the Spirit in him. In everything, he turns to prayer, so that he may involve God with him. The Scripture says, "The LORD will fight for you, and you shall hold your peace."[84] And the phrase "hold your peace" can only mean that you should not rely on yourselves.

The self-reliant person increases his works, but the God-reliant person increases his prayers. The self-reliant person boasts if he succeeds, but the God-reliant person gives thanks to God and glorifies Him if he succeeds. The one who relies on himself forgets God and uses his skills, capabilities, tricks, strategies, methods, and strength. As for the one who relies on God, he makes God his all in all, and perceives that his abilities, if it were not for God working in them, would amount to nothing, because "Unless the LORD builds

---

[83] Psalms 44, according to the Coptic text in 6th Hour of the Agpeya.
[84] Exodus 14:14.

the house, they labor in vain who build it."[85] The Lord has said, "Without Me you can do nothing."[86]

The self-reliant person is as far as one can be from obedience and seeking guidance. This is because he obeys no one but his own mind, and trusts no opinion besides his own. In all this, he depends on no one but himself, for he is wise in his own eyes. He sees that he knows everything, so why should he turn to spiritual fathers? Why would he seek anyone's guidance? What new thing could he get from them? And if he does sit with his father of confession, it is merely to get from him the approval for what he has already decided upon in his mind! And if the father indicates something to him, he argues with him a great deal, and would not easily accept an opinion from him. The same goes for his relationship with his physical father and other elders.

For this reason, the self-reliant person is headstrong and stubborn. How easy it is for him to disagree with others! He considers that anyone who disagrees with his opinion must be wrong. If he enters a discussion with someone, it is not easy for him to be persuaded; and thus were the heretics and innovators in the history of the Church. How many explanations and proofs did the fathers provide to them, and yet they insisted on their opinions because their self could not back down.

---

85 Psalm 127:1.
86 John 15:5.

In fact, the self-reliant person is stubborn even in his relationship with God Himself, and therefore, he cannot live a life of submission. He wants God to do for him all that he requests and all that he thinks is good for himself. He finds it hard to say to the Lord, "May Your will be done," and hence, just as he grumbles about people, he grumbles about God also! Just as he complains about people's treatment of him, he complains about God's treatment of him also, whether about answering his prayers, or about the manner of life which the Lord has chosen for him. This is because he constantly walks according to his own will.

The self-reliant person can never be humble. This is because the first principle of humility is self-denial. As for the person who is fought with the self (the ego), he constantly searches for his dignity, personality, and what he wants for himself, of rights, authority, or loftiness. If he possesses any glory, he constantly boasts about it, and if he does not, he constantly seeks all sorts of glory.

The self-reliant person is always righteous in his own eyes. He never condemns himself, and never admits that he has made a mistake, whether this admission be before God, people, or even before himself. And if the mistake which he made was obvious, he would try to shift the responsibility to someone else, as both Adam and Eve did,[87] or he would try to justify himself regarding the pressing surrounding circumstances.

---

87 See Genesis 3.

If he fails an exam, he attributes the reason to the difficulty of the exam, or that the grading was tough, or he may blame God who did not help him but rather abandoned him. But if he passes, he attributes this to himself, to his effort and intelligence.

The person fought with the ego tends to take more than he gives, and thinks that he builds himself up by constantly taking, through the strategy of collecting and hoarding. An example of this is the rich fool, whose ground yielded plentifully, and whose wealth increased, so he said, "I will pull down my barns and build greater, and there I will store all my crops and my goods. And I will say to my soul, 'Soul, you have many goods laid up for many years; take your ease; eat, drink, and be merry.'"[88] He did not think of his eternity, but about his self's enjoyment on earth, and the result was that he lost both eternity and the earth too, and was called "the rich fool."

Likewise, caring about the self may lead to stinginess. The one who wishes for his possessions to increase so that his self may enjoy them, finds it difficult to give. The Lord gave us the example of the rich youth who "went away sorrowful, for he had great possessions,"[89] as well as the story of that rich man who did not give Lazarus, the poor, the crumbs that fell from his table.[90] These rich people see that giving diminishes their money, which the self enjoys.

---

88 Luke 12:18–19.
89 Matthew 19:22.
90 See Luke 16:21.

Therefore, because of the self, they give neither tithes nor firstfruits. For the person fought with the ego does not merely say "I," but also says, "*my* money," "*my* possessions," "*my* projects." And he boasts that his money multiplies day by day. Meanwhile, giving tithes diminishes it, and the same applies to giving the firstfruits. Regarding this, divine inspiration says, "Will a man rob God? Yet you have robbed Me!"[91] The Lord said, "It is more blessed to give than to receive,"[92] because in giving there is love for others, and not a love for the self, as it happened with the widow who put in offerings out of her poverty.[93]

With regards to giving, we mention giving in general, and not only the giving of money. Giving can be done in the form of time, effort, and feelings. For the person fought with the ego is stingy with giving part of his time and effort to others, because in his care for his self, he wants all the time to be for this self, in contrast to the good Samaritan who, passing by a wounded man on the road, cared for him, and gave him of his time, effort, and money so that he may be healed.[94]

---

91 Malachi 3:8.
92 Acts 20:35.
93 Luke 21:4.
94 See Luke 10:25–37.

Chapter 4

The Ego is the Cause of Many Other Sins

The person who is constantly preoccupied with his self has neither the time to care for others, nor even the desire to care about the kingdom of God or the service of people. All that concerns him is "What will I be? How will I be? When will I be?" Not only is he not preoccupied with others, but he also wants the entire world to be preoccupied with him!

The likes of this person are exceedingly far removed from the [Church] service and its spirit. And if he joins a service, he does not serve with a spiritual aim, for the sake of building the Kingdom and the benefit of others, but he rather takes service as a means to build his self up, and as an opportunity to be seen and to practice what he is fond of: authority and leadership!

If the self enters a service, it ruins itself and the service too. And it may be an opportunity for authority and control, and so he says, "Nothing should be done without my permission, without my guidance and thought. The decision is my decision, and the management is my management, even if everyone agreed on something else." For this reason, he involves no one with him in the service except those who follow him and submit to him, and he does not mind getting rid of the rest so that he may be the sole worker, planning and executing.

This concerns the administrative aspect of service. However, the self may take another direction, namely, a personal thought in teaching, where he does not follow the Church's general teachings, but rather his own philosophy and his own interpretation of Scripture, and he spreads whatever he himself believes, even if it is a new thought that contradicts what has been handed down!

Many heresies throughout the history of the Church were formed from such a philosophy that comes from the self, from ideas which some invented, clung to, and spread. Sometimes, such people form particular clusters within the Church, each with its own thinking, direction, style, and isolation from the whole. It is the ego!

From the ego's dominion and stubbornness, divisions are born. Indeed, from where do wars and fights come except from the self? The ego causes familial disputes, which may get as far as courts and lawsuits, and what precedes these of discord, quarrel, or separation, where the person does not think about others' happiness or about pleasing them, but about his own comfort, his own dignity, and his own rights, whether this be within his family or in the Church.

And because of the ego, he builds his comfort upon the distress of others. Because of the self, the person focuses on himself and does not open up to others, and he clings to his thinking and attacks others' thinking. What matters is that he wins, even if at the failure and loss of others.

Therefore, he loses his love for others, and others' love for him because he lives within a narrow circle, that is, the circle of self. He sees himself as right, and everyone who contradicts him as wrong. He is right; others are wrong. Of course, with this, he cannot be a social person; for either he would withdraw into himself, or would clash with others. And he justifies himself by ascribing error to others. Thus, he turns others into fuel to warm himself up. They must see matters the way he sees them, even if [they have to see them] with a wrong perspective.

And he may belittle others so that he is always the best, thus falling into the sin of judging [others]. This may increase to the point that he falls into the sin of defamation, particularly against those whose success and excellence he envies. This is because he cannot stand the existence of anyone better than him, or of one who is praised more than him. And so, he is troubled [from dealing] with the people, and he troubles the people along with him.

The self-centered person is always difficult to deal with, because the person dealing with him is bound to be the losing party in every discussion and in every undertaking in which they partner with him. The people who deal with him will never reach a result with such an obstinate person who clings to his opinion; therefore, it is better for people who deal with him to stay away from him, for the sake of their peace of mind.

Even in his dealings with God, he is not easy [to deal with], firstly, because he does not seek the kingdom of God, but rather his own kingdom, and does not want God's will, but his own will. Even in his prayer, he does not ask for God's counsel, but imposes his demands on God, as if to say, "Lord, look at this matter that I present to You. I have studied it well, and all that is left for You is to carry it out for me, and to do this and that with it!" Not only does he ask God to carry out his will, but it must also be done quickly and without delay.

The self-confident person appoints himself as a supervisor over God's works with him. With pride, he argues with God, "Why did You do this to me? You were supposed to do that instead." And if God does not fulfill what he wants, he gets angry with God, and threatens to cut off all relations with Him and His Church, and to abstain from prayer, fasting, and the Eucharist.

If such are his dealings with God, then his dealings with his father of confession are even worse. Oh, how easy it is to disagree with him! And as a person wise in his own eyes, he may propose things to the father of

Part One: On the Ego

confession to receive the approval, and not for the sake of receiving advice. For he knows what is good, perhaps even more so than the father of confession! And it is easy for him to argue with the father of confession and make him out to be wrong. And how easy it is for him to abandon his father of confession and search for another father if his guidance is not according to his liking!

If the self-centered person reproaches someone, he does so mercilessly. He does not care about the feelings of the person whom he reproaches, but he wants to vent the feelings of distress within him. And his sense of honor may not accept any excuse or justification presented to him. His honor—in his view—is too great for excuses to wipe away the insult he feels!

Consequently, his anger may be severe and may turn into hatred, which may last long, because he does not forgive easily. And so, his self remains affected, and deeply so, for an extensive period of time until he feels that his self has received its due satisfaction, and his honor has gained the appreciation it desires. Therefore, in his anger, he may blow up and become furious in defense of his self, its dignity and its rights.

He may not be satisfied with only becoming angry, but may even resort to revenge. Without a doubt, all crimes of vendetta are a result of the self expanding its circle to include all members of the family, village, sports team, and so on. He takes revenge to get justice for himself or his relative, and for the honor of the family. Revenge does not just mean murder; rather, he may try to ruin others by any means. It may also include gloating over them if they suffer a loss from another source.

The person fought with the ego finds it difficult to cooperate with others, because he wants everything to be his, or the larger share to be his, whether from a profit or management standpoint, or people's praise. To him and the other applies the expression said in the Book of Genesis: "Now the land was not able to support them, that they might dwell together."[95]

There may be two servants working together in one church who are unable to live together, despite them being some of the most senior servants. This is also because of the self, wherein caring for the service vanishes, and the self remains! Who is more important? For whom do the privileges belong?

One day, a servant entered into a deep discussion about a church-related issue with a senior servant. This senior servant became furious with him and said to him, "You ought to know who you are, and who I am." This servant, the more junior one, came to me to complain about what was said to him, so I said to him, "The most appropriate response would have been to say to him, 'We are both dust and ashes, just as our father Abraham said about himself.'"[96]

Sometimes the person might not be prominent, but through daydreaming, he imagines for himself

---

95 Genesis 13:6.
96 See Genesis 18:27.

an image of prominence and greatness. These dreams are a form of self-magnification through imagination. They are a portrait of a soul unsatisfied by the reality in which she lives, and so resorts to satiating herself through daydreams. And so, she imagines that she has become so and so, and has done such and such a thing, and has gained all sorts of glorification and respect from people! Daydreams are involved in the wars of vainglory, and the person lives through them in an illusion that makes him happy, all the while forgetting and neglecting to remember that he does not have the ability to attain his dreams and illusions.

How easy it is for a person who is fought with self to become hostile. He would take a hostile stance against all those who stand in the way of this self, or oppose it, or compete with it—or against anyone whom he thinks is doing so. And he would wage a brutal war on them, a war that knows neither peace nor conscience. And if he happened to know something old about this person, he would announce it and expose them, and heap on accusations against them, all so that his self remains unchallenged and unresisted.

For the sake of defending the self, he does not mind lying and hypocrisy. The self is the cause of lying, because when the self errs, and the person wants to conceal its errors (so that it may appear blameless before others), he lies to cover up its flaws and deficiencies. Or he may lie to fulfill a certain purpose for his self, or in the pursuit of a sinful desire his self desires for him, for a friend, or for a foe.

ON THE EGO & THE LOVE OF PRAISE

Likewise, for the sake of the self, the person resorts to trickery and craftiness. And because of the self, he resorts to hypocrisy, so that his self may appear virtuous before others, and so that it may receive praise from them, thus receiving its wages on earth.[97]

Often, the ego stands in the way of consecration. An example of this is the mother who stands in the way of her son's or daughter's monasticism by refusing, pressuring, crying, or illness, to carry out her opinion and wishes, which are for her child to be near her and not to become consecrated as a monastic, or she may pressure them to marry a spouse she picks. And in all this, she does not care about their hearts' feelings and their desire to consecrate themselves to God, but rather it is the self that is pushing the mother into carrying out her thought, even if she sacrifices her child and their spiritual joy.

Another example is a mother getting involved in her son's marital life. She does not mind separating him from his wife, or him treating his wife harshly or coldly, to please her. And if he does not do this, the mother accuses him of being an ungrateful son who forgot her labor in raising him, or she may say that he is a weak husband whose wife influences him and makes him submit to her! In all this, she is not concerned with the failure of his marital life as much as she is with his obedience to her. It is the ego!

---

[97] See Matthew 6.

Also, the person who loves his self may become persistent to the point of annoying and troubling others. He wants to carry out his ideas or desires by all means and with all swiftness, and hence he resorts to extreme insistence that gets on others' nerves. And this is done by repeating his request, and pressuring people into doing it now, as is, regardless of the obstacles that may prevent this, and regardless of how inappropriate the situation may be. The ego, however, wants! And it does not care about embarrassing the one it asks. And it becomes difficult to deal with this pushy person who cares about nothing but his self.

And the self and ego include selfishness with all its intricacies, whereby the person is self-centered, and thinks of nothing but of it [the self], that it should have all its desires, and for the sake of this, he favors it over all. For if his self clashes with a person, he favors his self over his love for this person, and if it is in conflict with some principles and values, he sacrifices all principles and values for the sake of his self, but even if his self clashes with the love of God, he favors it over God and His love.

Indeed, isn't every transgression against God caused by the self?

Isn't the self the cause of the loss of every virtue?

The self that rejects humility and pursues the first places; the self that suffers from conceit and thinks of itself more highly than it ought to;[98] and that desires

---

98   See Romans 12:3.

to perform miracles and speak in tongues, so that it may become elevated in the eyes of others; the self that loves self-righteousness and pushes the person into being righteous in his own eyes, wise in his own eyes, and great in his own eyes, and in the eyes of others; the self that favors itself over everyone and builds its comfort on the distress of others; the self that finds its pleasure in falling into all carnal and material lusts, thus defiling its body, which is the temple of the Holy Spirit; the self that favors itself over God by sin and loves being independent of Him in its thinking and conduct—thus the self leads to the loss of the soul.

What is the cure, then?

Chapter 5

He who Loves His Life will Lose It

Thus did the Lord say in the Gospel of St. John, "He who loves his life[99] will lose it, and he who hates his life in this world will keep it for eternal life."[100] By this, He means that he who loves his life with a wrong love will lose it. As for the phrase "he who hates his life," what is meant is that he does not give his self all that it desires. Rather, he has the virtue of self-control, and so he does not let it walk according to its whims, but restrains it from its desires if said desires are contrary to God's commandments. By this restraint, he "will keep it for eternal life."

The phrase "hates his life" was repeated in Luke 14:26, where the Lord says, "If anyone comes to Me and does not hate ... his own life also, he cannot be My

---

99 "His life" in the Arabic verse is literally "himself" or "his soul." Henceforth, when this Arabic phrase is used by Pope Shenouda in the text, it is either translated into "his life" or "his self."
100 John 12:25.

disciple."[101] Hence, this is a condition for discipleship unto the Lord. However, can a man even do this?

All people love themselves. There is nothing wrong with this, since the divine commandment says, "Love your neighbor as yourself."[102] However, what is true love of self? True love of self is to preserve the self's purity and cleanness, and to never allow it to be separated from God by sin, but to love God with all the heart and all the mind.[103] And true love of self is an exercise in spiritual growth, until it arrives at the life of holiness and perfection, according to the Lord's commandment, "be perfect."[104] Meanwhile, some, in building themselves up, resort to erroneous methods that destroy them!

The first erroneous method of love of self is giving it its pleasures and enjoyment. If its enjoyment were spiritual, this would be good. However, the error lies in giving it pleasure through the senses, carnal, material pleasure that does not benefit it; rather, this carnal pleasure leads it to lust and to sin: "the lust of the flesh, the lust of the eyes."[105] And this carnal love may lead to the pleasures which Solomon fell into when he said, "Whatever my eyes desired I did not keep from them,"[106] desire for possessions, money,

---

101 Luke 14:26.
102 Matthew 19:19, 22:39.
103 See Matthew 22:37.
104 Matthew 5:48.
105 1 John 2:16.
106 Ecclesiastes 2:10.

luxury, and women, until he finally realized that all of this was vanity and grasping for the wind. A carnal love of self may prevent a person from fasting, and may also prevent them from keeping vigil, as well as preventing them from being pure in body.

The one who entertains his self with the pleasure of the flesh and the senses, rather causes it to be lost, and forgets that "the world is passing away, and the lust of it."[107] He also forgets the parable of the rich fool who thought, in his love of self, of gratifying it with many goods laid up for many years, saying to it, "Take your ease; eat, drink, and be merry."[108] Similar to him is Lazarus' rich man, who on earth received his good things,[109] and by that he lost the eternal comfort. He also loved his life, and so lost it. Indeed, everyone who desires, in his mistaken love of self, to give it the pleasures of the world, the luxury of life, the delights of the earth, and the enjoyments of the senses, will lose it.

Some derive pleasure, not through the senses, but through the mind. What he does not realize through action, he gains through thought. To enjoy anything he wants to, it is sufficient for him to close his eyes and come up with tales, stories, imaginations, and daydreams, and he takes pleasure in all this. And he says to himself: "I will become… and I will be… and I will do… and I will enjoy…" And he may drown in this thinking for hours.

---

107 1 John 2:17.
108 Luke 12:19.
109 See Luke 16:25.

Those who are deprived in their practical lives compensate themselves with thoughts and imagination. They enter into the pleasure of daydreaming. As the common maxim goes, "The hungry dreams of the bread market." So too does the person wander in imagination. Take a student who did not study, for example. They may abandon their book and swim in many thoughts: They have passed and excelled, and have gotten accepted into a prestigious university, and have graduated and become this and that—then they wake up from their daydreams, only to find that they wasted time in them, time which they desperately needed for studying.

Imagination is a type of enjoyment, much greater than that of the senses. This is because the scope of thought and imagination is limitless, and much wider than that of vision, hearing, and the rest of the senses. Through this imagination, people come up with scenarios that could never happen in reality. Therefore, he who loves to delight his self through imagination, sedates it, and when it wakes up, it finds itself empty.

Perhaps this is what happens in patients suffering from megalomania, also known as delusions of grandeur. This topic brings to my mind a story that happened nearly half a century ago. A few medical students went on a visit to a psychiatric hospital to observe patients openly. They saw one of them claiming to be a prophet sent by God. And he was standing, inviting people to believe in his message. When they were done listening to him, they saw another patient next to him, calmly sitting in silence. So they asked him, "Why weren't you listening to the speech of the prophet of God?" So he said to them, "Don't believe his claim that he is God's prophet, for I never sent him!"

And so, there are people who think that, in the love of self, they equip it with greatness. They think that they fulfill themselves through grandeur, the prime example of this being the Devil, who said, "I will ascend above the heights of the clouds, I will be like the Most High."[110] And with the same grandeur, he fought our first parents, saying to them, "Your eyes will be opened, and you will be like God."[111] An example of this is also those who wanted to build the Tower of Babel, saying, "Come, let us build ourselves a city, and a tower whose top is in the heavens; let us make a name for ourselves."[112] All those who loved their self with a wrong love, through grandeur, caused themselves to perish: whether Satan, or Adam and Eve, or the builders of the Tower of Babel. For those who loved their lives through grandeur and hence lost them, their purpose was worldly greatness, and not spiritual greatness.

For a person arrives at spiritual greatness through humility, as the Lord said, "For everyone who exalts himself will be humbled, and he who humbles himself will be exalted."[113] Therefore, he who loves himself with a true love ought to flee from haughtiness:

---

110 Isaiah 14:14.

111 Genesis 3:5.

112 Genesis 11:4.

113 Luke 18:14.

"For the day of the Lord of hosts shall come upon everything proud and lofty…. The loftiness of man shall be bowed down, and the haughtiness of men shall be brought low; the Lord alone will be exalted in that day."[114] We have an example of this in King Herod, who, because of grandeur, was struck by the angel of the Lord and died, and was eaten by worms.[115] He also loved his life through grandeur and so lost it.

The one who loves their life through grandeur may enter into wars and conflicts that ruin them. An example of this is Absalom, the son of David, who wanted to exalt himself by seizing his father's throne while he was still alive. Consequently, this desire led him to wage war against his father, and to defile his father's bed, and the result was that he died in sin and perished.[116] He also loved his life—with wrong love—and so lost it.[117]

This is in contrast to St. John the Baptist, who humbled himself and so was exalted. He continually said, "He who is coming after me is mightier than I, whose sandals I am not worthy to carry."[118] He also said, "I indeed baptized you with water, but He will baptize you with the Holy Spirit,"[119] and "It is He

---

114 Isaiah 2:12, 17.
115 See Acts 12:22–23.
116 See 2 Samuel 16:15–20.
117 "His life" in the Arabic verse is literally "himself" or "his soul."
118 Matthew 3:11. Also see Luke 3:16.
119 Mark 1:8.

who, coming after me, is preferred before me, whose sandal strap I am not worthy to loose,"[120] and "He must increase, but I must decrease. He who comes from above is above all."[121] This John, who was above the level of the ego, is the one whom our Lord Jesus Christ described as the greatest among those born of women.[122]

How beautiful is that which was said about God, in this regard, that "Who is like the Lord our God, who dwells in the highest, and who looks upon the humble things in heaven and on earth?"[123] The humble creatures are those that are far from the ego.

Other people try to build their self up through an appearance of domination in their own eyes, or through "heroism" that employs the approach of conflict and battle. You find him like a flame of fire, always eager to criticize, demolish, and destroy, without taking any positive, constructive action! Instead, you hear nothing from their mouths except the phrases "this is wrong" and "he/she is wrong," and they take pleasure especially in criticizing people who are their seniors. Their ultimate role model is Tarzan, who leaps across mountains and beats this and that person. They are no different from boys who love movies that involve gunfire, flipping cars over, and destruction and murder, which they call hero movies.

---

120 John 1:27.
121 John 3:30–31.
122 See Matthew 11:11.
123 Psalms 112:5–6 LXX, OSB.

Each of these views himself as a hero when he says, "I will bring down so-and-so," and "I will ruin so-and-so!" and "So-and-so will not escape my hands! I'll show him who's boss!"

It is what they call "a fiery temperament," constantly attacking, always hostile, always angry and invasive, building his own grandeur[124] upon the skulls of others. And he finds his pleasure in destroying others. His self, which he loves in this way, he loses, and while he believes that he destroys others, he destroys himself, and gains neither this world nor the hereafter.

He is like the mischievous student in class. He thinks that he will attract attention to himself by making trouble, but in the end, he ruins himself, while success is the portion of his calm, mild-mannered classmate. He feels good about himself when he annoys the teachers, and he does not bother with respecting them, believing what he is doing to be boldness, strength, and bravery. But with all this, he sentences himself to ruin, and the verse applies to him that says, "he who loves his life will lose it."

This type you will find everywhere: in the field of service (unfortunately), in social circles, and in the field of work. These people say, "I am a fighter!" They do know how to fight, but without realizing where these fights will lead them.

What is striking is that destruction is easier than construction—and faster. As the common maxim

---
124 Literally: elevation.

says, "The well that a wise man digs in a year, a fool can plug in a day!" It is easy for a twenty-floor building to be demolished by an evil person in an hour, or in moments, with an explosive bomb. And so, construction remains a glorious work. As for those who demolish, they demolish no one but themselves.

There is another type: [those] who love their self by granting it freedom in everything. They do whatever they want, whenever they want, however they want! This happens in some Western countries. Once the child reaches adolescence, no one has any authority over them: no authority for the parents, nor the teachers, nor do they acknowledge any leaders or guides. They think that advice is a shackle, and traditions are a shackle. Neither orders nor instructions are allowed to restrain their freedom, and through freedom, they lose their life! They say, "I'm a free person! I'm free to do whatever I want!" And the word "I" brings about their ruin.

True freedom is freedom on the inside, not in external actions. True freedom is the liberation of a person from the habits that enslave them, and their liberation from their whims, desires, lusts, and sins. As for the corrupt [understanding of] freedom, many a time has it led youth to smoking, drugs, gambling, and moral corruption. It leads them to ruin from all sides, and hence "he who loves his life will lose it."

Existentialists think that they will find themselves by being liberated from God and His commandments. And their slogan has become, "It is better that God is not, so that I am!" Truly, this ego is what ruins them. He who loves his life loses it.

Likewise is the parable of the prodigal son,[125] who perceived that the ego's enjoyment and freedom are [realized] in him leaving his father's house and walking according to his whims. And the matter ended with him saying, "How many of my father's hired servants have bread enough and to spare, and I perish with hunger."[126]

There is a vast difference between freedom and unruliness. People think that they are breaking out of the forts, which protect them, into the vast expanse, wherein lies their doom! The confessant also thinks that they are breaking out of the chains of guidance from their father of confession, and so they reach unruliness in their actions, and the unruliness ruins them. And so they only consult their father of confession on matters they are sure that he will agree on, but in other matters, they walk according to their will. Or they may change their father of confession, so that their ego may walk as it pleases!

Those who believed they were fulfilling their self through freedom caused them to perish due to their poor use of freedom. True freedom—the undistorted liberty—does no harm. However, what does harm a person is the freedom that turns into a form of unruliness, in which lies their doom.

---

125 See Luke 15.
126 Luke 15:17.

Part One: On the Ego

One of the most dangerous types of freedom is freedom of religious thought. Many have been led by this freedom into atheism, or into establishing their own religious ideologies within the Church, or have been led, through their freedom in interpreting the Holy Scriptures, into heresy and heterodoxy, especially when the ego is involved, where the deviant person cherishes their erroneous thinking and clings to it; and they find it contrary to their dignity to back down from their incorrect interpretation and heresy.

All of the manifold sects that have caused division within the Church are caused by the ego. You could argue with some of these people, and even though the Holy Scripture's verses are clear, they would still reject them.

They do not submit to the Scriptures, but rather they want the Scriptures to submit to their thinking! Each one interprets the Scriptures according to their own inclination, but inclinations vary, and therefore, the interpretations vary, and various sects arise. Some find their self's fulfillment in proposing new, bizarre interpretations no one has beaten them to, and this type of interpretation brings about fame for them, by which they imagine that they present their self as intelligent, intellectual, and innovative. The Church finds itself preoccupied with responding to them, and they find pleasure in the fact that the Church is preoccupied with them. It is the ego that causes them to deviate, all so that they may be seen and become famous in the field of knowledge—the knowledge of which Scripture said that it "puffs up."[127]

Each of these satisfies his self in that he is an intellectual leader and possesses a novel thought. He does not have ordinary thought like everyone else, but rather he has a novel, ingenious thought, even if it were a heresy! What does heresy mean, except that its owner has innovated, inventing a new thought that is unfamiliar? And this innovator—in his love of self—is delighted when he is said to be the originator of a such-and-such thought, and the founder of a new doctrine that some people embrace! And if you ask him, "Why don't you walk according to the known doctrine of the Church?" he responds by saying that he is a thinker and that he offers his ideas for the benefit of others! And thus, since he loves his life, he will lose it, as he resists the Church, and the Church resists him also, and she may even remove him from her membership because of his heresy.

Another person may love himself and thus fall into being infatuated with himself. He is wise in his own eyes, and righteous in his own eyes, and if he does not find people to praise him, he praises himself, and speaks about the wonderful and virtuous deeds he has done. Even if he has flaws, he tries to justify them to appear flawless before all. He has no qualms with everyone else being mistaken, while he is the only one of sound opinion.

---

[127] 1 Corinthians 8:1.

And therefore he falls into arrogance, which ruins him. If he is punished for a mistake, he accuses the person punishing him of being unjust, because he is righteous, and the righteous should never be punished! He does not look to the offense he has committed, but instead complains about the harshness of whoever punishes him. He has a special mirror by which he sees himself other than how people see him. He believes that he is worthy of praise from everyone. If people praise someone else, he gets hurt on the inside, as if they had ignored him!

Cain was hurt by God's acceptance of Abel's sacrifice,[128] so he killed him, despite that Abel had not harmed him in any way. Those who fall into the love of self and its praise, and into self-conceit, lose their life through pride.

Others love to build themselves up with external honor: with status, wealth, fame, and pride of life. All these do not lead to true honor. For the true honor of the self is in its purity and its fellowship with the Holy Spirit. It was said about John the Baptist that he was "great in the sight of the Lord,"[129] not only great before men. And perhaps this greatness of his was that he was "filled with the Holy Spirit, even from his mother's womb."[130]

---

128 See Genesis 4.
129 Luke 1:15.
130 Ibid.

External greatness, however, does not build a person, but may cause his perdition, for it is connected with people's view of him, and not with his relationship with God. How easy it is for those who delight in status, fame, wealth, and grandeur to have the [following] words said to them: "you received your good things"[131] or "they have their reward."[132]

External appearances do not build the soul; rather, the fruit of the Spirit builds it. The fruits of the Spirit are the living bricks by which you build yourself, about which St. Paul the Apostle said, "But the fruit of the Spirit is love, joy, peace, longsuffering, kindness, goodness, faithfulness, gentleness, self-control."[133] So, are these fruits in your life? And as for worldly positions and ranks, they are not what will get you into the Kingdom.

Do not seek honor from men, for Christ the Lord said, "I do not receive honor from men."[134] What, then, is the honor He sought? He said, "O Father, glorify Me together with Yourself."[135] It comes by self-denial with respect to people, and the Lord started it in the story of redemption in that He "made Himself of no reputation."[136]

How, then, do we forsake the self?

---

131 Luke 16:25.
132 Matthew 6:16.
133 Galatians 5:22–23.
134 John 5:41.
135 John 17:5.
136 Philippians 2:7.

Chapter 6

How to Eliminate the Self (the Ego)

We can get rid of the domination of the self through the following means.

1. Conquering the Self

Fasting and chastity are involved in conquering the self in the sense of controlling the requests of the body and its desires. And there is another conquering of self when it comes to the desires of the soul. For the soul may desire the love of appearances, to announce itself, and to seek greatness. In all this, we must resist it, for joyful is the person who guards their soul and prevents it from straying after worldly comforts, and persuades it that finding comfort in God is better.

If your soul or body inclines to the enjoyments of this world, fiercely forbid them, not out of harshness against them, but to guarantee your eternal life, for he who pampers his self here loses it.

He who is lax in controlling his self will be overpowered by it, and it will rebel against his spiritual conduct, in contrast to the one who trains his self and tames it in the paths of the Lord.

The way, with which you may build your self up, is to conquer it and overcome it, because by conquering the self and overcoming it, you attain the true glory of self, which is other than the external appearances of greatness, pleasure, and fame; all of these are external things, whereas the psalmist sings in the psalm, "All the glory of the daughter of the King is within."[137]

Trust that in conquering the self lies a spiritual delight unparalleled by all delights of the flesh. For this reason, if you want to build your self up, conquer it with regard to its external yearnings, so that you may build it on the inside, whereupon you will find it in God, and will find God in it, and you will see it ascending toward eternity.

From here, we see that asceticism is one of the ways of treating the ego. In asceticism, you build your self up, not in this present world, but in the coming world. For as Joseph the righteous stored up wheat for coming years, you also should store up that which will benefit you on the day you stand before the Just Judge. And as the wise virgins stored up oil for the time when the Bridegroom came,[138] you also store up oil of the work of the Holy Spirit in you. Conquer your self in

---

[137] Psalms 44, according to the Coptic text of the Agpeya.
[138] See Matthew 25.

the things of the world, because the world is passing away, and the lust of it.[139]

If your self wants to triumph over others, conquer it, because true victory is victory over the self. As for others, instead of triumphing over them, win them over, because the Scripture says, "He who wins souls is wise."[140] Triumphing over people is easy, but winning people over is what requires effort, if you conquer your self in it.

2. Loving Others and Serving Them

Break out of the prison of your self within yourself, to the circle of others. The psalm says, "Bring my soul out of prison."[141] What imprisonment is harsher than imprisoning yourself within this ego? Come out of it, then, and integrate into the outside world, with others whom you love, serve, and cooperate with.

Indisputably, the person who loves his self does not care about the love of others. Try, then, to come out of focusing on caring about yourself to caring about others. Be assured that you will find delight in this, and they will love you back, and you will find in their love what will satisfy your soul.

Move from the realm of taking to the realm of giving. Train yourself in giving others: offering them service, giving them time, giving them love, effort,

---

139 See 1 John 2:17.
140 Proverbs 11:30.
141 Psalms 142:7.

and assistance. For when a man grows in the practice of giving, he will give even himself. This is the loftiest [degree] he reaches in becoming released from the self.

And if one of the errors of the ego is stinginess, then the treatment is giving, where the person trains to always have an open hand, extended in giving to others with generosity, compassion, and tenderness. Their gratitude will satisfy him, and helping them will change his heart and fill it with noble emotions, making him give more, and he will increase in serving others and in making them happy.

And he will get accustomed to laboring for the sake of others. He will not care about his own comfort, but about the comfort of others, in contrast to the selfish person who builds his comfort on the distress of others. And as the spiritual person grows in caring about the comfort of others, he may arrive at the life of consecration, because the consecrated person is he who offers his whole life for the sake of others.

3. Humility

The person who lives within the love of the ego cares that his self constantly enlarges; and in comparison [with others], he desires for it to be higher than theirs. The treatment for this is to set before himself the apostle's words: "In honor giving preference to one another."[142] Regarding this, the Spiritual Elder says,

---

142 Romans 12:10.

"And wherever he happens to be, may he become little and a servant of his brothers."[143] But [even] the Lord Jesus Christ says, "If anyone desires to be first, he shall be last of all and servant of all."[144] In this way, he practices the virtue of "the last place."[145]

What is meant by "the last place" is not to be last with respect to place but with respect to status. Therefore, do not consider yourself the most important in whatever place you are in, nor that your opinion is the most important opinion, nor that your decisions are the most important decisions, nor that your position is the most important. And do not think that you have to be the one obeyed and respected among all [around you]!

Do not give yourself honor, nor impose it on others; rather, let people honor you for what they see in you of humility and meekness. Do not force people to respect you, because respect springs from within the heart; it is not imposed by force, but is [given] by personal appreciation. You may force a person to obey you, but you cannot force them to respect you.

And in your dealings with people, be a breeze, not a storm. Many people love the character of the storm because it carries the meaning of power. The breeze, however, represents meekness and kindness, both of which the one who denies himself ought to be

---

143 *The Letters of John of Dalyatha*, Hansbury M.T., trans. (Piscataway, NJ: Gorgias Press, 2006), 88.
144 Mark 9:35.
145 Literally: the last seat.

characterized by. And in your humility, do not favor yourself over others, provided that this is done with deep love and humility, and without hypocrisy.

In your humility, say, "I? Who am I? I am merely dust and ashes. But before I was dust, I was nothing. God created the dust before me, and then created me from this dust." Here, self-esteem will vanish away from you. And in your humility also, you will attain the virtue of self-condemnation.

4. Self-condemnation

The person suffering from the ego is always righteous in his own eyes. If he makes a mistake, he does not apologize because he thinks that he is right and has not made a mistake. And if a misunderstanding arises between him and another person, he does not go to them to be reconciled, because he expects that the request for reconciliation must come from the other side, considering that the error originated from the other side and not from him. But even with God, he might not confess his sins, because his own self persuades him that he has not sinned!

The treatment, then, is for the person to hold themselves accountable without partiality, and to condemn the self: to condemn it within himself, to condemn it before God and before the father of confession, and to condemn it before others when it is necessary.

He should condemn it in humility and not cast blame on others, as our father Adam and our mother Eve did.[146] And he should not justify himself with respect to the reasons for the mistake and its circumstances, for all the reasons for justification are caused by the self and its holding onto its self-righteousness.

The person who does not apply himself to glorifying his self and magnifying it, but rather constantly aims at purifying his self of the sins and deficiencies that taint it, you will find him blaming his self and condemning it, because by this he can straighten it and correct its course.

Once, Pope Theophilus visited the area of the Cells, and asked the Abba, the guide on that mountain, about the virtues which they had acquired, so he answered, saying, "Believe me, father, there is nothing better than for a man to cast blame on himself in everything."[147]

This is the spiritual method by which a man seeks to correct his self: to cast blame on himself, not on others, nor on the surrounding circumstances, nor on God, thinking that God did not provide him with the necessary assistance!

If only we condemn ourselves here, so that we may escape condemnation on the last day! For by

---

146 See Genesis 3.
147 Cf. *Give Me a Word: The Alphabetical Sayings of the Desert Fathers*, Wortley J., trans. (Yonkers, NY: SVS Press, 2014), Theophilus 1.

condemning ourselves, we draw closer to repentance, and through repentance, the Lord forgives us our sins. As for he who does not condemn his self due to his admiration for the self, he will continue in his sins, and will not change for the better, and will be under condemnation. How true were the words of St. Anthony the Great when he said, "If we condemn ourselves, God will be pleased with us. If we remember our sins, God will forget them for us, and if we forget our sins, God will remember them for us."

Likewise, our self-condemnation helps us in our reconciliation with other people. It is sufficient for a person to apologize and say to his brother, "You are right. I have sinned in this matter," to put an end to the anger of the person who was wronged and to be reconciled with them. If, however, the person at fault continues to justify his position, the opponent will intensify their condemnation against him. How beautiful is the saying of St. Macarius the Great: "Judge yourself, my brother, before they judge you."[148]

5. Set the Example of Christ Before You

If the first human was defeated in the war of the self and desired to be like God,[149] then the Lord Christ, who blessed our nature in Himself, corrected this point.

---

148 *Bustan al-Rohban al-Mowasah, al-joz' al-Awal* [The Expanded Paradise of the Monks, Vol. 1]. (Egypt: St. Macarius Monastery, 2006), 268.
149 See Genesis 3:5.

How so? The Apostle says that He "made Himself of no reputation, taking the form of a bondservant, and coming in the likeness of men."[150]

And He lived on earth as a poor person, having no place to lay His head,[151] without an official job in society. And He waived His honor, "He was oppressed and He was afflicted, yet He opened not His mouth…. And He was numbered with the transgressors."[152] And He did not defend Himself.

He denied Himself for our sake, humbled Himself to raise us, and stood as one who is guilty so that we may be justified. He did not set His self before Him, but He set us. Is this not a lesson for us from He whose greatness is boundless? A lesson for us—we who are fought with the ego, while we are nothing! The Lord Jesus Christ emptied Himself of the true glory, whereas you empty yourself of every vain glory.

6. The Second Mile Exercise

The Lord said, "If anyone wants to sue you and take away your tunic, let him have your cloak also. And whoever compels you to go one mile, go with him two."[153] In the same manner, the Lord spoke about the other cheek, saying, "Whoever slaps you on your right

---

150 Philippians 2:7.

151 See Luke 9:58.

152 Isaiah 53:7, 12.

153 Matthew 5:40–41.

cheek, turn the other to him also,"¹⁵⁴ as if He wanted to say, "Be the wronged, not the one who wrongs, and be the crucified, not the crucifier. Do not avenge yourself." The self wants to take justice for itself and to take it by itself, here on earth, and as fast as possible, whereas the Lord's teaching to us on self-denial is to "not to resist an evil person."¹⁵⁵

Do not let your self intervene to receive your rights or to take revenge, and remember the Scripture that says, "'Vengeance is Mine, I will repay,' says the Lord."¹⁵⁶ Even though vengeance is the Lord's, do not request it from Him for yourself. Rather, the Scripture says that love "does not seek its own."¹⁵⁷ And why does it not seek its own? Because it is far from the self, far from the ego that seeks [its own].

7. How the Saints Used It

The prophets, the apostles, and the saints used the word "I" within the realm of humility and contrition of heart.¹⁵⁸ Abraham, the patriarch, whom God blessed and made a blessing,¹⁵⁹ saying to him, "And in you all the families of the earth shall be blessed,"¹⁶⁰ we find

---

154 Matthew 5:39.
155 Ibid.
156 Romans 12:19.
157 1 Corinthians 13:5.
158 Literally: contrition of soul.
159 See Genesis 12:2.
160 Genesis 12:3.

Part One: On the Ego

him, with regard to the word "I," say, "I who am but dust and ashes."[161]

And David the prophet, who had great boldness with God, and through whom God had performed a great victory over Goliath,[162] we find him after this, when they offered him to be King Saul's son-in-law, say to them, "Does it seem to you a light thing to be a king's son-in-law, seeing I am a poor and lightly esteemed man?"[163] And how abundant are his confessions of his weakness in the psalms, when he says, for example, "Have mercy on me, O LORD, for I am weak."[164]

And John the Baptist, despite being the greatest among those born of women,[165] said to the Lord, "I need to be baptized by You,"[166] and he said to the people, "One mightier than I is coming, whose sandal strap I am not worthy to loose."[167]

And the great apostle Paul, who was caught up to the third heaven,[168] said about the Lord Jesus Christ's appearance to the apostles after the Resurrection, "Then last of all He was seen by me also, as by one born out of due time. For I am the least of the apostles,

---

161 Genesis 18:27.
162 See 1 Samuel 17.
163 1 Samuel 18:23.
164 Psalms 6:2.
165 See Matthew 11:11.
166 Matthew 3:14.
167 Luke 3:16. Also see Matthew 3:11.
168 See 2 Corinthians 12:2.

who am not worthy to be called an apostle, because I persecuted the church of God."[169]

This is the sound usage of the word "I," in a spirit of contrition.

In the same spirit, the great saint Paul the Apostle sends to his disciple Timothy, saying, "Although I was formerly a blasphemer, a persecutor, and an insolent man; but I obtained mercy because I did it ignorantly in unbelief."[170] He says this about himself in a letter to his disciple, whereas the custom is for teachers to boast in front of their students. However, he used the word "I" in a sound way.

And we notice that when he spoke about his being caught up to the third heaven, he did not say "I," but said, "I know a man in Christ."[171] Therefore, he did not use the word "I" for glorification, but used it when confessing his errors.

Regarding glorification of the self, the fathers took care to glorify it in heaven and not on earth. Regarding the ego's glory on earth, in this brief, present life, they dreaded the Lord's saying about those who receive praise here from people, "Assuredly, I say to you, they have their reward,"[172] and the same expression was repeated in Matthew 6:16. In the same sense, our father Abraham said to rich man in the story of Lazarus

---

169 1 Corinthians 15:8–9.

170 1 Timothy 1:13.

171 2 Corinthians 12:2.

172 Matthew 6:2.

the beggar, "Son, remember that in your lifetime you received your good things."[173]

As for those whose wages are great in heaven, they are those who concealed the word "I," and practiced virtue in secret, before their heavenly Father who sees in secret and who will reward them openly;[174] likewise are those who used the expression "not I" and similar phrases.

8. "Not I"

An example of this is St. Paul the Apostle, who, regarding his successful ministry, said, "But by the grace of God I am what I am, and His grace toward me was not in vain; but I labored more abundantly than they all, yet not I, but the grace of God which was with me."[175] Here, we focus on the phrase "not I, but the grace of God which was with me."

The apostle Paul repeats the same understanding, saying, "I have been crucified with Christ; it is no longer I who live, but Christ lives in me."[176] It is not I who work, but Christ who is in me does everything. I, however, have been crucified with him. I have crucified the word "I" so it no longer appears.

Likewise, all servants who do not desire that the ego receive glory should say, "Not unto us, O LORD,

---

173 Luke 16:25.
174 See Matthew 6.
175 1 Corinthians 15:10.
176 Galatians 2:20.

not unto us, but to Your name give glory."[177] Indeed, when it comes to glory, each of us should say, "Not I; not unto me."

And this is the same conduct that St. John the Baptist followed. For he rejected all glory directed at him, at the ego, and redirected it at the Lord Jesus Christ, uttering his timeless phrase, "He must increase, but I must decrease."[178] How frequently did the Baptist repeat the expression "not I" or "I am not," but I am merely "the friend of the bridegroom, who stands and hears him, rejoices greatly because of the bridegroom's voice. Therefore this joy of mine is fulfilled."[179]

Not only should we say the expression "not I" with respect to our relationship with God, but also with respect to our relationship with each other. For, with respect to honor, each one of us ought to say, "not I," fulfilling the apostle's commandment, "In honor giving preference to one another."[180]

And with respect to leadership, each one of us also ought to say, "not I," fulfilling the commandment of the Lord who said, "Whoever desires to become great among you, let him be your servant. And whoever desires to be first among you, let him be your slave."[181]

---

177 Psalms 115:1.
178 John 3:30.
179 John 3:29.
180 Romans 12:10.
181 Matthew 20:26–27.

And in the expression "not I," we follow the Lord's commandment regarding the last place; we leave the first places for the scribes and Pharisees who desire them.[182] And if they are offered to us, we say, "Not I, but my brother is better than me, and it is more appropriate for him." And thus we live the life of humility.

---

[182] See Matthew 6:23.

Chapter 7

"Not I"

1. Self-Denial

So did St. Paul the Apostle say: "I have been crucified with Christ; it is no longer I who live, but Christ lives in me."[183] My self does not live at all; I have hammered nails into it; I have crucified it. I have disposed of the dominion of the self. I no longer think of it. I have given it up for the sake of the Lord, and for the service of my brethren. But how marvelous is his saying, "For I could wish that I myself were accursed from Christ for my brethren, my countrymen according to the flesh."[184]

It is the [same] self-denial which the Lord has called us to, a condition of following Him, for He said, "If anyone desires to come after Me, let him deny himself, and take up his cross, and follow Me."[185] What St. Paul did for the sake of his brethren and

---
183 Galatians 2:20.
184 Romans 9:3.
185 Matthew 16:24; see also Mark 8:34.

countrymen according to the flesh is the same as what Moses the prophet said to the Lord in intercession for the people: "Yet now, if You will forgive their sin—but if not, I pray, blot me out of Your book which You have written."[186]

But [even] the Lord Jesus Christ—glory be to Him—started His Incarnation with the same principle, since it was said about Him that He "made Himself of no reputation, taking the form of a bondservant, and coming in the likeness of men. And being found in appearance as a man, He humbled Himself and became obedient to the point of death, even the death of the cross."[187]

This is the Master Lord who said to the Father, "Your will be done,"[188] "not as I will, but as You will,"[189] and also said, "because I do not seek My own will but the will of the Father who sent Me."[190] He repeated this in John 6:38. Through all this, He teaches us a lesson.

How marvelous this is, that even the Lord Jesus Christ says, "not I, not my will, not what I desire." He says this despite His unity of will with the Father! By the Lord's saying, "If anyone desires to come after Me, let him deny himself," He has made self-denial the beginning of the path. What, then, is its end?

---

186 Exodus 32:32.
187 Philippians 2:7–8.
188 Matthew 26:42.
189 Matthew 26:39.
190 John 5:30.

Some Examples

Our father Abraham, the patriarch and the father of the prophets, began his calling with the principle of "not I." He began by obeying the word of the Lord, "Get out of your country, from your family and from your father's house, to a land that I will show you."[191] "Yes, Lord, it is not I who would choose my dwelling place, nor would I cling to my country, family, or house." So he went after the Lord, "not knowing where he was going."[192] "It is not I who would ask to know where I am going. It is sufficient that You guide my steps."

Jeremiah the prophet attained this experience when he said, "O LORD, I know the way of man is not in himself; it is not in man who walks to direct his own steps."[193]

Our father Abraham also practiced the phrase "not I" when he took his only son to offer him as a burnt offering to the Lord.[194] "It is not I who would cling to my feelings as a father, nor would I argue with You on Your wisdom and command; all that I shall do is obey, and may Your will, O Lord, be done. Do You desire to take from me this son for whom I have waited for long years according to Your promise? May what You desire be done, not what I desire."

Moses, the prophet, experienced the phrase "not I" also, he who lived as a prince in Pharaoh's palace.

---

191 Genesis 12:1.
192 Hebrews 11:8.
193 Jeremiah 10:23.
194 See Genesis 22.

He said to himself, "It is not I who should live in such grandeur and luxury while my people are enslaved." But he "refused to be called the son of Pharaoh's daughter, choosing rather to suffer affliction with the people of God than to enjoy the passing pleasures of sin, esteeming the reproach of Christ greater riches than the treasures in Egypt."[195]

The phrase "not I" was experienced by the Lord's disciples and apostles. They left ships and [fishing] nets, kin and family, and followed the Lord.[196] Matthew left the tax office and followed Him.[197] Saul of Tarsus left the authority and his Pharisaism and followed Him. St. Peter the Apostle expressed all of this when He said to the Lord, "See, we have left all and followed You."[198] It is as though each of them were saying, "Not I, but Christ. Not my family, nor my house, nor my ship, nor my occupation, but Christ, He for whom I forsake everything."

And in the same vein, St. Paul the Apostle said, "But what things were gain to me, these I have counted loss for Christ. Yet indeed I also count all things loss for the excellence of the knowledge of Christ Jesus my Lord, for whom I have suffered the loss of all things, and count them as rubbish, that I may gain Christ and be found in Him."[199]

---

195 Hebrews 11:24–26.
196 See Matthew 4:20.
197 See Mark 2:14.
198 Matthew 19:27.
199 Philippians 3:7–9.

2. Self-Denial in the Service

Man must practice the phrase "not I" in the service, making God his aim and means in the service. The person should not seek personal glory, but should sing that beautiful phrase with the psalmist in the psalm, "Not unto us, O LORD, not unto us, but to Your name give glory."[200]

This is the principle that the saints lived by in the service. An example of this is St. John the Baptist, who disappeared so that the Lord may appear, and who carried out the phrase "not I" in his service, and said, "He must increase, but I must decrease."[201] "'I am not the Christ,' but, 'I have been sent before Him.' He who has the bride is the bridegroom; but the friend of the bridegroom, who stands and hears him, rejoices greatly because of the bridegroom's voice. Therefore this joy of mine is fulfilled…. He who comes from above is above all."[202]

The ego was entirely non-existent with John the Baptist, he who, when they praised him, or thought he was the Christ, responded with "not I." "I am not the Christ…. There stands One among you whom you do not know. It is He who, coming after me, is preferred before me, whose sandal strap I am not worthy to loose."[203]

---

200 Psalms 115:1.
201 John 3:30.
202 John 3:28–29, 31.
203 John 1:20, 26–27.

But the people who are defeated before the ego are the opposite of this, for how easy it is for a servant to get the people he serves attached to his person and not to God. Or he may have a group among them who follows him and defends him no matter how much he errs, who praises him and glorifies him, who is hostile toward those who are hostile toward him, and who follows him even if he falls into heresy, just as the followers of Arius followed him in his heresy. And so the Arians became a threat to the Church that lasted longer than Arius himself. Here, we see the self clearly.

Those victorious over the ego are not like this, however. Service, to them, is an honest attempt at entering the depths of the soul to purify it and draw it nearer to God, by forsaking its sins, and by loving God and goodness. So also was the language or approach [in the service]. The aim of the service is a spiritual one. It is a ministry of reconciliation to God.[204]

There is a great difference between a sermon from which the listeners go out, saying, "What an erudite speaker!" and one from which they go out, saying, "We want to repent and to be reconciled to God." The aim of a sermon is not the glorification of the speaker, but the salvation of souls. The successful speaker is he who wins over souls to the Lord, whose aim is not his own self, seeking for it personal esteem from his listeners.

---

204 See 2 Corinthians 5:18, 20.

The aim of a sermon is to reveal to the listeners their self, and the flaws that are in it, how to triumph over it and to draw closer to God, and how to be reconciled to God and abide in Him; and the aim of a sermon is not to present information to the listener, their ignorance of which they will not be judged for on the last day.

If every speaker purified himself from the self, and purified his sermon from caring for his self, and focused it on the salvation of others, we would then win many souls over to the Kingdom. If only all servants were like John the Baptist, preparing the way before Christ, and making ready for Him a prepared people.[205]

There are two things by which the service becomes successful, one that is far from the self, and these are:

1. God being the aim, and also the means.

2. The self not being an aim, nor a means.

We say this because many have the appearance and glorification of the self as an aim of their service, and their means in the service is the reliance on the self, its intelligence, and its abilities. Consequently, God is not included in the service, while it was supposed to be God's service! And so also, prayer diminishes in the service; thereby it becomes weak because God has not blessed it nor is working in it. Or He has not participated with the servants in their service.

---

205 See Luke 1:17.

If the self gets involved in the service, division might occur in it between servants, with one becoming Paul's, and the other Apollos'.[206]

With the word "I," the love of authority and the love of superiority enter the field of service, which is why the Lord forbade them from this, saying to them, "Yet it shall not be so among you; but whoever desires to become great among you, let him be your servant.... just as the Son of Man did not come to be served, but to serve, and to give His life a ransom for many."[207]

3. Self-Denial in Prayer

Through the principle of "not I," the Lord taught us to first seek the kingdom of God and His righteousness, telling us about material things that "after all these things the Gentiles seek. For your heavenly Father knows that you need all these things. But seek first the kingdom of God and His righteousness, and all these things shall be added to you."[208]

And when He taught us the Lord's Prayer, He made our first requests be about God, as though the person praying were saying, "Not I," but "our Father in heaven, hallowed be Your name. Your kingdom come. Your will be done on earth as it is in heaven..."[209] Then, after this, they mention other requests belonging to

---

206 See 1 Corinthians 3:3–4.
207 Matthew 20:26–28.
208 Matthew 6:32–33.
209 Matthew 6:9–10.

the kingdom of God and His righteousness in it, like the spiritual bread specific to the kingdom of God, the request for the forgiveness of sins so that they may be reconciled to God; and that God may deliver us from the evil one, so that through them [that is, the requests] we may arrive at the purity of God, to become worthy of the dwelling of God within us.

There are other prayers which contain no personal requests at all, but are rather meditations on God's beautiful attributes, like the Trisagion: "Holy God, Holy Mighty, Holy Immortal," and "Holy, Holy, Holy, Lord of Sabaoth, heaven and earth are full of Your holy glory," and like many other prayers in the Liturgy of St. Gregory, where the person praying says, "You are He whom the angels praise and the archangels worship.... You are He whose glory the authorities declare. You are He unto whom the thrones send up honor. Thousands of thousands stand before You and ten thousand times ten thousand offer You service. You are He whom the invisible bless and the visible worship..." They are all prayers to which the phrase "not I" applies.

The prayers of praise are followed by the prayers of contrition, in which we seek what God desires of us, and where the self apologizes to Him for its mistakes, and it appears sinful, humiliated, and not great or proud. Its prayers may be accompanied by prostrations, where it bows itself to the ground, confessing its sins and regretting them. It does not lift itself up, but rebukes itself before Him.

The highest degree of prayer is the prayer of praise, where man pushes his self to the side, and mentions nothing but God, meditating on His greatness and glory. Prayers of contrition and prayers of thanksgiving come after, in which there is also glorification of God.

4. Forget Yourself

In the principle of "not I," forget yourself, and remember God alone. In your entire practical life, say, "not I, but the grace of God which was with me."[210] Neither my knowledge, nor my power, nor my intelligence, nor my mind, as the apostle said, "But we have the mind of Christ."[211] He also said, "It is no longer I who live, but Christ lives in me."[212] Tell the Lord, "I do not govern myself, but You govern me. I do not rely on my understanding, for Your commandment says, 'Lean not on your own understanding.'[213] It is not I, also, who can repent through my struggle, but rather You 'restore me, and I will return.'"[214]

I forgot myself a long time ago when I began living the life of submission to You. But [even] my whole life is Yours, in which I sing with the apostle, "For to me, to live is Christ, and to die is gain.... having a desire to

---

210 1 Corinthians 15:10.
211 1 Corinthians 2:16.
212 Galatians 2:20.
213 Proverbs 3:5.
214 Jeremiah 31:18.

depart and be with Christ, which is far better."[215] And for the sake of this, say also, "Nor do I count my life dear to myself."[216]

And trust, my brother, that with the phrase "not I," you can enter the Kingdom. For when you deny your self, renounce your self, and even hate your self for the Lord's sake, you will all the more cling to God. Not only will God be the first in your life, but He will be all the more the only One. And when you say "not I," you will move far from the glorification and magnification of the self, and you will escape the praise of the self, boasting, pride, and vainglory—those things which many have fallen into. And you will attain a life of humility by which you can draw close to God, for the Scripture says, "But [God] gives grace to the humble."[217]

And when you say "not I," you will give preference to others in honor, according to the commandment,[218] and will take the last place, from which God will elevate you. But you will [even] be loved by people, because you will not compete with them in superiority; neither will you crowd them on life's path, but you will rather give them an opportunity to advance.

When you say "not I," you will not flatter your self, or justify it, or make excuses for it. But, on the

---

215 Philippians 1:21, 23.
216 Acts 20:24.
217 James 4:6.
218 See Romans 12:10.

contrary, you will rebuke and chastise it, and you will also accept the Lord's discipline and not complain, "for whom the LORD loves He chastens."[219]

Oh, many are the virtues that we acquire by the phrase "not I!"

---

[219] Hebrews 12:6.

PART TWO
ON THE LOVE OF PRAISE

Chapter 1

Degrees of Sin in the Love of Praise

Being praised is one thing, and the love of being praised is another. For a person may be praised and not sin. However, if they love praise, they have sinned. Our fathers, the apostles, were praised. The great saints and martyrs were also praised, but they did not sin. For the sin is not in hearing praise, but rather the sin is in loving this praise that you hear.

There are two types of people who are not fond of praise. The first is a type that flees from any praise approaching them, whether that praise be from people, demons, or themselves. The second type goes to great lengths to flee from praise and honor, to the point where they impute many flaws to themselves, and expose their own follies and deficiencies, undermining their worth in front of people, even if it leads to things being said about them that are not so.

Degrees of Sin in the Love of Praise

The First Type: A person who is praised without seeking praise. When praise comes, they are pleased and rejoice. They did not seek it, but as soon as praise arrives, they are pleased. This type contains subtypes:

1. A person who is pleased with praise, and hears it in silence as they sit quietly, internally pleased, without anyone else sensing their joy.

2. A person who hears praise and prompts its escalation. In other words, they continue to say things that make the person who is praising them praise them further, like drawing them from one topic of praise to another which they can be praised on, or otherwise employing any other means that makes the person in front of them increase their praise.

3. A person who loves praise and is pleased while hearing it, but pretends that they are unhappy, despite being internally pleased. They continue to resist so that the other person may praise them even more, without the actual intention of finding fault with themselves. Rather, deep within themselves, they want to hear nice words.

The Second Type: A little more problematic is the person who has not received praise and yet still hungers to hear it. In their desire, they follow one of two paths:

1. They desire praise and remain silent until it reaches them, devising grounds for people to praise them, such as opening up a particular subject so

that they may be praised for doing something in this subject, or inching the conversation step by step until it reaches the point with which they are pleased, so people can then praise them for it.

2. A person who desires praise and performs righteous deeds before people so that they may praise them.

The Third Type: There is an even more problematic type than this, for they love praise and long for it, and yet find that praise does not come despite their waiting and despite coming up with excuses for people to praise them. They therefore reach a different level, where they hate those who do not praise them and consider them enemies, and misunderstandings arise between them. Truly, this person did not harm them, save for not praising them with a few sweet words, or not meeting them pleasantly, or not offering them excessive respect, or not dignifying them in a special way. The likes of this person, who hate those who do not praise them, what then will they do to those who criticize them? If the simply silent person who does not praise them is hated, how then will they feel about their critics?

The Fourth Type: There is another type that desires praise, who is pleased when they hear it, who hates those who do not praise them. They are not satisfied with just this, for they praise themselves when they find no one to praise them, and so they speak of the virtuous deeds they have done that are deserving of praise while concealing their own sins. These people are those who excessively speak about themselves.

The Fifth Type: There are even more troublesome types than those who praise themselves, for self-praise is of two degrees. In the first degree, the person praises themselves for who they *are*, i.e., they keep talking about the glorious deeds they have done and their virtuous traits. In the second degree, the person praises themselves for who they *are not*, attributing to themselves virtues they do not possess, or exaggerating and magnifying good traits which they have, or attributing others' deeds to themselves. For example, if you participate in a good work and then tell the story, you might not say that you were just a participant in a good work, so that you would be the only one praised. However, you might inflate this a little and focus all the work on yourself, as if all the others who also took part with you have no existence and have not expended any effort.

Sometimes, it goes a step further, where you attribute a great number of flaws to others, accusing them of negligence or weakness, burying their share in the work. You might untruthfully say, for example, that a person was unable to speak, and that they kept stuttering until people were upset at them, at which point you intervened and said the correct response. This implies that *you* were the master of the situation, and *someone else* erred. Not only did such a person praise themselves, but they praised themselves and slandered others too.

A saintly monk used to deny himself very much such that when he would do a good work, knowing that people would praise him for it, he would involve someone else with him in the work, even if in a very small capacity, or at the end of the work, he would ask someone to help him. This way, if he were asked about the work after its completion, he would say, "May God bless so-and-so who did this work," giving him the credit to keep the praise of people away from himself.

There is another clear example of the love of praise: that is, soccer. If a team with a love of praise is playing, they will all fail, for they will all hog the ball, each wanting to score a goal on his own, but will lose the opportunity. Meanwhile, a different player might initially run the ball close to the goal line on his own, but then pass it to one of his teammates, resulting in a goal, after which the latter is praised despite him doing nothing, while the first person did everything. If such is the case with sportsmanship, how much more should it be with respect to spirituality?

This type of person, who praises themselves, ignoring all surrounding circumstances and the people assisting, ascribing everything to themselves, obliterates God's right in this work, for they forget God's part. They forget the circumstances that facilitated the success of this work, and focus everything on themselves, and praise themselves for who they are not.

The Sixth Type: This is considered the worst degree of the love of praise, where a person's love of being praised may reach such a point that they love to be praised exclusively, and are upset if others are praised. They wish to be the only person praised, no one else. If another person is praised, they envy them, become jealous of them, speak ill of them, and hate them.

Chapter 2

Evils that Result from the Love of Praise

1. Hypocrisy: The lover of praise becomes a hypocritical person who does not present a truthful image of himself; he conceals the dark spots within himself, and only displays the bright ones. In trying to conceal the dark spots, the person advances gradually in many directions; as too in displaying the bright ones, he advances gradually to grave points, and so the person falls into innumerable mistakes.

2. Intolerance and Anger: So long as the lover of praise conceals his flaws, he will consequently not accept being confronted with his faults; therefore, he is someone who hates criticism, and who, if criticized, cannot bear it. It may not just stop at intolerance, but gradually it progresses to anger, agitation, irritability, outbursts, and so on, to the end of this road. For how dare a person criticize him? And how dare they say one bad word about him? And how dare they mention a specific fault to him? And he rages and seethes and becomes troubled inside and out, and troubles others with him too. All of this is because of the love of honor and praise. It is here that we must realize that the cure for many types of anger is for a person to not be a lover of honor and praise, for much of our anger is due to a love of praise, whereby a person cannot bear an insult, or a word of criticism, or an offensive remark.

3. Hatred: The lover of praise hates those who do not praise him, and also hates those who criticize him, and hates those who praise others in front of him.

4. Envy: The love of praise and honor is one of the foremost, fundamental causes of envy, for the envious person desires to take the place of others, and he does not like for others to be better than him.

5. Criticism, Condemnation, Defamation, and Insulting Others: For he loves distorting others' work so that all may be found to be inferior to him, and only he be found better. He falls into condemning others by exposing them, and falls into cursing and the like of undermining the rights of others.

6. Losing People's Love: He loves no one, and no one loves him.

7. The Lover of Praise Loves the First Places (Matt 23:6, Luke 11:43): He loves grandeur, and fights with people over these first seats, and enters into struggles and creates problems with others: Who will be first? Who will lead? Who will have authority? Who will be in the spotlight? If anyone else desires to be seen, he feels that he must put this person down to the bottom and call them inferior.

8. Lying: By this, he falls into lying. He feels there is no problem with a lie if lying will lead him to being elevated and recognized.

9. He Create Conspiracies and Schemes to eliminate the people who are prominent out of his way, so that he alone remains.

10. The love of praise leads to even more than this. It leads a person to wish for the death of others so that he may take their place. He desires the destruction and loss of others to take their positions, like when there is an agent at work who desires the job of his superior by any means possible. He wants them to leave their job, and he requests their death from God, so that he may be promoted to their place, and he requests that their superiors get angry with them, or that false words may be said about them, all so that they may be shoved aside and their place be made vacant for him. Perhaps his conscience does not permit him to speak a word against this superior. However, he waits with an abundance of patience for any bad remark to be said about them, and is exceedingly pleased and rejoices when it comes, even if this rival of his is not at fault. He does not excuse them or defend them despite his knowledge that they are not at fault, and he cannot testify to the truth that would serve their interests.

11. The love of praise and honor does not merely render a person unable to endure discipline, rebuke, and humiliation, but it also makes him unable to bear words of advice, for how could someone else advise him? Is this other person better than him? Do they understand better than he does when *he is* the knowledgeable, the learned, the instructor, the mentor, the guide? The matter may even escalate to the point where he cannot stand one person advising another in front of him, for only he may give advice and guidance; it is an insult to his dignity! And he gets upset and angry, and no one understands the reason because he is boiling on the inside. If he is asked about the cause of his anger, he is unable to give a reason. Through this, he creates a problem for himself and others.

For instance, if a question is posed to another in his presence, or if people respect another in his presence to the extent that he feels that the respect directed at others was more than that which was directed at him, he gets upset and becomes troubled inside, even if for a simple reason like a person entering and greeting other people with more longing and respect than him.

Therefore, this person, this lover of praise, grows weary. He is unable to tolerate people, and, in this case, people cannot tolerate him either.

12. The love of praise and honor also makes a man unstable: it puts one in an indecisive state, lacking in stability, having no principles, opinions, or plans. Why? Because they do not walk according to principles, but rather walk with the goal of [being] praised. If a matter brings praise, they do it, and if its opposite brings praise, they do the opposite.

For he changes color with people,[220] no matter what their character[221] is. With dignified people, he is dignified and balanced, and with the jesters, a jester he becomes. So, where did this previous dignity and balance go? Has it ended, because "to everything under heaven is a time"? With the lovers of chatter, he speaks the entire day so that he may be praised, and with the lovers of silence, he is silent so that he may be praised. If he finds that the truth and its defense procure him praise, he will defend it, and if this defense angers people, he will not say the truth lest he anger them, and the praise be gone. He wants praise and nothing more, by any method and by any means, and he does not mind changing color with people to arrive at praise. In front of those who love asceticism, he does not eat, and to those who love pleasure, he serves many varieties on the dining table. With him, each occasion has its own clothes, and for each person, he assumes an image, a form, and a behavior. Before the people who love humility, he sits in a dignified manner, with humility, and does works for which he can be praised as humble; and before the arrogant, he too takes on their image, so that he may be praised.

---

220 I.e. like a chameleon.
221 Literally: image.

He is a multi-colored person who does not persist in any one state, so that he may receive praise. He lives in misery and anguish; he loses his inner peace. He longs for honor, and if it does not come to him, he becomes troubled and miserable, but if it does come, he rejoices and is pleased. He is momentarily pleased, but misery accompanies him, for he longs for greater honor, and lives in weariness because this greater honor has not arrived. This matter does not end, and his misery continues with them always.

13. The lover of praise falls into arrogance, haughtiness, and pride, and these lead him to the rest of the evils.

14. Finally, the lover of praise suffers a complete loss of his spiritual life, for all the virtues that he does are thoroughly distorted when the love of praise mixes with them, corrupting them. He ends up with no virtues at all, for every virtue he possesses has become distorted due to the corruption of the aim and motivation behind them, which is the love of praise.

This person, no matter how hard he works and toils, stands before God empty-handed. He has no reward with God, because he has received his wages on earth.

For God will say to him on the last day, "You have received in your lifetime on earth your good things of praise, honor, and greatness, and do not deserve a thing with Me in Heaven. What do you deserve? Did you toil and do virtuous deeds? You did not do virtuous deeds for the Lord, but for praise, for yourself, and for your own elevation," so you have no reward with God.

Thus, this person loses heaven also, and the eternal kingdom, and God. In his struggle with people and his love for honor, he loses the people also, because people do not like the arrogant, the haughty, the multi-colored, or the lover of praise. Rather, he subjects himself to others' contempt and disdain when he praises himself in front of them.

St. Isaac the Syrian said: "Honor flees away from before the man that runs after it; but he who flees from it, the same will it hunt down."[222]

---

[222] *The Ascetical Homilies of Saint Isaac the Syrian*. (Boston, MA: Holy Transfiguration Monastery, 2011), 166.

Chapter 3

How does a Person Flee from the Love of Praise and Honor

1. Hiding Your Virtues and Good Deeds

To flee from the praise of people, I must hide my virtues and good deeds. This does not mean that I should not do anything good, but that I should not do it in front of people with the intention of being praised. If this deed must necessarily be done in front of people, and I am unable to hide it, then the aim, at the very least, should not be the people, but the deed itself.

St. Augustine addressed this issue in his interpretation of the Holy Scriptures. The Holy Scripture says, "Take heed that you do not do your charitable deeds before men, to be seen by them. Otherwise, you have no reward from your Father in heaven."[223] In another place, the Scripture says, "Let your light so shine before men, that they may see your

---

223 Matthew 6:1.

good works and glorify your Father in heaven."[224] So, is there a contradiction between the two statements?

St. Augustine explains: "There is no contradiction because the fault lies not in people seeing your good works, but in performing good works with the intention of being seen by others."[225] Therefore, you must do good whether people see you or not. Your aim should not be for people to see you, nor to praise you. Do the good work, not to be glorified yourself, but for God to be glorified, so that they may glorify your Father in heaven.

Some say that they do good to be "good examples" for others. However, let us understand well that "good examples" are situation-dependent. For there are people who, by virtue of their position, are obligated to be good examples, such as clergymen, leaders, people in charge, the apostles, and the prophets, because these, if they were not good examples, would cause others to stumble.

As for the humble person, they do not set themselves as examples, for they do not see anything within themselves that people ought to emulate. They try to flee from the situations of being good examples with the excuse that they are sinners and wretched, and on the contrary, they lay bare their own deficiencies and weaknesses. Despite this, they may still become good examples in their humility. However, they do not desire this, and so weep before God and say, "O Lord,

---

224 Matthew 5:16.
225 See Augustine, *Sermons on Selected Lessons of the New Testament* Sermon IV. (NPNF[1] 6).

I am a hypocrite. You know of the rotten bones inside the whitewashed tombs. All my deeds are evil. You have covered me and hid my flaws from others—shall I then take advantage of this cover to be an example? I am a sinner, and I have no good deeds." This is the humble person. This person may reveal their flaws to flee from the praise of men.

But as for those who want to become examples, to appear good in front of people, they may fall into pride and hypocrisy. We must please God, not men, and so our aim should not be that we become an example, even if we become an example through God's arrangement.

In this manner did the holy fathers abandon the practice of a certain virtuous matter if it became known, and they would do another, for they fervently fled from praise.

However, this does not mean that you ought to quit every good course you walk in so that you may not be harmed. Rather, hold fast to every righteous practice for the sake of your spiritual life, and not so that people may see you.

2. Avoiding Positions of Authority and Offices

A. It is because they are a danger to man, and it is better for the wise to flee. Let us mention as an example the story of St. Pinufius, whose story St. John Cassian related,[226] the founder of monasticism in France.

---

226 See John Cassian, *The Institutes* IV.XXX–XXXI. (NPNF[2] 11).

Part Two: On the Love of Praise

St. Pinufius was the abbot of a monastery housing 200-300 monks in the area of Burullus. He was very humble and revered, and had a standing with many who loved him because of his holiness and his virtuous life, and for his great gifts that God had granted him, and for his priesthood. Because he was a venerable elder, this saint sat with himself one day and said: "What will the result of this matter be? Every day is praise, honor, respect, and veneration. I fear that God will come to me on the last day and tell me that I have received my good things on earth. Where is the narrow and difficult way, doing according to the verse that says: 'We must through many tribulations enter the kingdom of God,'[227] while I am a man enjoying respect and veneration and honor and a high rank?"

For this reason, St. Pinufius fled from the monastery one day without anyone noticing, disguising himself in layman's clothes, and walked south until he reached one of the monasteries of St. Pachomius the Great in Esna. He knocked on the door, asking them to accept him into the monastery, so they looked at him with disdain. Who is this old man who has come to become a monk? And they said to him, "You came after you have enjoyed the pleasures of the world, and have had your fill of it, and it has had its fill of you. Shall you then come in the last days to become a monk and to make [yourself] a saint? You are not fit; begone from us!" Then St. Pinufius importuned them, but they refused and said to him, "You are an old man, and

---
227 Acts 14:22.

you cannot endure monasticism and its struggles." He continued to importune them and stood at the door for a while despite their refusal, without food or drink. When they saw his endurance and patience, they took him into the monastery under the condition that he would not be consecrated a monk and would remain in layman's clothes, serving in the monastery. They charged him with assisting the young monk responsible for the monastery's garden—to be his underling. He did not mind, and the youth took to giving him orders to do, and he was obedient and submitted to him, and the saint whom everyone used to respect and obey turned into a disciple. But it was his wish, for he wanted to change his inner life, and submit to others, and not have others submit to him. His teacher, the young monk, was very harsh in temperament, desiring to discipline the elder correctly, for monasticism is not laziness. The saint obeyed him with perfect obedience and carried out his orders with all precision, without arguing or debating. He continued according to this course for a while, and the youth was pleased with him.

He also used to wake up in the early hours of the night, when all the monks were asleep, and perform the tasks that others found repulsive because of their filthiness. So when they woke up in the morning, they found that everything had been done, but they did not know who had done it, and so they would rejoice and glorify the Lord for it. As for him, he was pleased by this work and persisted in this manner of life for three years, saying, "I thank you, Lord, for Your gifts and great blessings, for here there is no respect, no esteem, no veneration, rather obedience and orders."

After this, a monk from the monasteries of Burullus came to visit this monastery and saw St. Pinufius carrying manure and placing it around the trees, so he doubted himself and did not believe that it was him. Finally, he heard him recite the psalms in his usual voice, so he recognized him and bowed before him, thereby revealing the matter. And they received him with great glory and took him back to his monastery.

After that, he fled again to Bethlehem and worked as a servant in John Cassian's cell, and it so happened by coincidence that another monk was going to visit the Holy Land, and when he met him, he recognized him, so they took him back a second time with respect to his monastery. St. John Cassian visited him when he came to Egypt and wrote about him in his works. He was a living example of fleeing from positions of authority.

He who wants to be saved from people's praise and honor must flee from positions of authority and offices, for they do not save the soul on the last day. Do not, therefore, search for positions of authority and offices, for they make you feel that you are something to yourself. If you succeed in them, the love of praise and honor will creep into you, and if you fail in them, perhaps you end up falling into much judgment.

B. The Dreams of Being in a Position of Authority: An Inner Trouble

Many a time does a person sit alone with themselves and daydream, imagining themselves in a grand position, doing this and that. Great projects and important matters revolve in their minds, and they think that if they were given authority, they would do what others cannot.

These fantasies of vainglory and pride are present within, which make a person feel as though they were capable of much. God may allow this person to be entrusted with a responsibility, which they then fail in, in order for them to realize the extent of their weakness.

Once, one of the elders went to visit a young monk in his cell, and as he was about to knock on the door, he heard a voice from inside. Waiting a little so as not to interrupt the young monk, he heard him preaching inside, so he waited until he had finished his sermon, dismissed the catechumens, and told them to "Go in peace." Then, he knocked on the door, and the young monk opened it, surprised by the elder in front of him. He was embarrassed and thought of what the elder would say about him if he had heard him preaching alone in his cell without there being catechumens, so he said to him, "Forgive me, Abba, if you have come a long while ago and have been waiting at the door." So the elder smiled and said to him, "I came, my son, while you were dismissing the catechumens," and thus this elder knew that this monk was being fought with vainglory, imagining himself to be a great deacon among those who teach and preach to the catechumens.[228]

Be cautious of imagining yourself as a leader, a ruler, or an adviser, or imagining that you are doing great things. Perhaps God will permit your failure so that you feel that you are weak and that you do not know anything, or perhaps you will become a leader and fall into the same mistakes that others have fallen into.

C. Positions of Authority are Harmful for the Immature

Abba Orsisius,[229] one of the successors of Abba Pachomius, said, "Positions of Authority are harmful to those who are not mature," and he gave an example of this, saying, "If you bring a brick that has not yet been fired in the fire and cast it into the water, it will disintegrate. However, if it has been fired in the fire, then when it is cast into the water, it will hold fast and be reinforced." Likewise, the person who falls into the love of authority before they are mature, before they are tested by fire, that is, with life experiences, before vainglory fades from them, is susceptible to destruction. Likewise, how unfortunate those are who submit to a leader who loves vainglory, for he destroys himself and destroys people with him for the sake of the glory that he seeks from them.

---

228 See John Cassian, *The Institutes* XI.XVI. (NPNF² 11).
229 See *Give Me a Word: The Alphabetical Sayings of the Desert Fathers*, Wortley J., trans. (Yonkers, NY: SVS Press, 2014), Orsisius 2.

D. Desiring a Position of Authority to Do Good is a Right-Hand Attack

St. John of Lycopolis was questioned regarding this matter. They said to him, "Is it fitting for a man to ask for a rank and authority to straighten the crooked and abolish evils?" He answered, "No, for if a man, even while away from rank and authority, is puffed up and loves grandeur, how much more will his conscience become haughty if he rises to authority? And if he, even while far from status, desires to become great, then what shall he do when he attains leadership and greatness itself? For he who did not know humility in his wretchedness, what then shall he do when he is in his greatness? And if he is puffed up even while far from high positions, what will he do when he takes up these positions? And if, despite having no reason for greatness, he wanders in his mind[230], how much more when he gains a reason to be proud? Therefore, if you do not desire the degree of humility, do not seek the degree of pastoral care. And if there is no pride in you, then do not desire the rank of the priesthood, for God takes care of His people more than you. Desire to be a sheep in Christ's flock, and not a shepherd from whose hands He will demand His flock's blood. Desire to be a lamb in the flock, guided[231] by others, rather than to be responsible for a flock. If you are unable to win your soul now, how then will you be able to win many souls? Remember death and the end of every person,

---

230 Literally: conscience.
231 Literally: shepherded.

Part Two: On the Love of Praise

and do not desire authority. Remember that no matter how honored with greatness you are today, tomorrow you will become like all men, imprisoned in the grave. If you, during the time you had no burdens on you, were unable to revive yourself, then how would you be able to save a great many people from the evils of this world? If you, now, without great responsibilities, were unable to save this one soul, that is, yours, how would you fare with people's souls?"[232]

Years ago, a youth who was recommended for the priesthood came to me and asked for my opinion, so I said to him, "My brother, when you become a priest, what will you do?" So he answered, "I will strive to save souls." I said to him, "Have you been able to save your soul so that you may save others'? Your soul, about which you know everything: You know all her secrets, her entire history, her weaknesses, the reasons behind these weaknesses, the flaws within her, and her maladies. If you are unable to save this soul, which is very well known to you, how will you be able to save the souls of the people with whom you will sit for short periods of time, whom you know very little about? Your soul, which accepts your rebuke if you rebuke it, you were powerless to save, so how then would you be able to save others who would get upset with you if your words were severe? Your soul, which trusts you and is ready to hear from you, you are

---

[232] Cf. *al-Aba'a al-Hathiqon fi al-Ibada, al-Joz' al-Thani* [The Fathers Experienced in Worship, Volume 2]. (Scetis, Egypt: Monastery of the Syrians, 2005), 207–208.

incapable of overcoming, so how will you work with people who may not listen to you and may doubt your words? Therefore, care first for the salvation of your soul, for the salvation of others is not easy."

The person who wants to save himself does not think of becoming a shepherd, but flees from shepherding as much as he can. If God firmly takes hold of him and he becomes a shepherd, then he will ask Him for power with which to do the work, for he, on his own, can do nothing. He who trusts in his own power, talents, and ability to save others is a very arrogant person indeed.

Let man stay away from the love of authority, even if the reason is a desire for people's salvation, because in reality, the reason is a love of vainglory, not people's salvation.

E. Fleeing to the Lowest Place[233]

The humble person distances themselves from positions of authority and offices, and loves the lowest place because they feel that this is what they deserve, as the saints have said, "Consider yourself least of all and last of all so that you may be at rest." St. Barsanuphius said, "Let us become foreigners, not counting ourselves as being anything, so that no one counts us as anything; and then we shall find rest."[234]

---

233 See Luke 14:7–11.
234 *Barsanuphius and John* 1, Chryssavgis J., trans. (Washington, D.C.: The Catholic University of America Press, 2006), 69.

The person who is not a lover of praise and honor flees from offices and first places, desiring to serve others and not to be served by anyone. He desires to be a disciple of a guide, not to be a guide to others. The Spiritual Elder said, "And wherever he happens to be, may he become little and a servant of his brothers."[235] One of the priests asked me for a word or advice after his ordination, so I said to him, "Be a son among your brethren, and a brother among your sons," because whoever goes down one step will go up many steps; this is the one who will be at rest in a high position.

As for the one who wishes to bask in all the dignity of this position, and fill their chair or be puffed up, this person is poor. But you, be last of all, the smallest of your brethren and their servant in every place you set foot in. If the Lord Christ washed the feet of the disciples, even though He is the Teacher and Master, should you then be a leader over anyone?

F. If You are a Leader:

This talk does not mean that I should reject leadership if it comes to me naturally, for the harm is not in leadership, but the love of leadership. The harm is not in becoming a leader, but in lording it over people. A person can become a leader and hold a first seat while being a humble person who treats people with the utmost gentleness, because he feels that he is one

---

[235] *The Letters of John of Dalyatha*, Hansbury M.T., trans. (Piscataway, NJ: Gorgias Press, 2006), 88.

of them. A leader is not a leader over individuals, but a leader over the work only. The leader and those led are equal before God, and those led may even have a higher rank.

A true leader is one who feels that he is a co-worker dealing with his subordinates in love and simplicity, for leadership and authority are given to people for the sake of managing the work, and not for the sake of their personal dignity. For example, if someone who receives a high priestly rank considers that a magnification of himself, he has strayed from the original purpose of authority, that is, a means of allowing the person in charge of the work to manage the work.

It is related that St. Pachomius, the father of monks, was once walking with a group of monks, each carrying his own belongings. One of the monks went ahead to carry St. Pachomius' belongings, but he refused and said to him, "If Christ, glory be to Him, called Himself a brother to the disciples, would I use you for my needs? This must never happen. Because of this, the other monasteries are in disarray, for their elders enslave their juniors."[236]

St. Paul the Apostle said, "These hands have provided for my necessities, and for those who were with me."[237]

---

236 *Bustan al-Rohban al-Mowasah, al-joz' al-Thani* [The Expanded Paradise of the Monks, Vol. 2]. (Egypt: St. Macarius Monastery, 2006), 87.
237 Acts 20:34

G. Be a Ruler Over Yourself First

The Spiritual Elder advised the young monks not to desire leadership in the assembly of monks, saying, "But if they greatly annoy you, answer them with submission and reliance on your Lord: '…My assembly is the gathering together of my thoughts and my passions. Concerning this, it is right for me to be made superior, ruling well the inhabitants of my house.'"[238] Therefore, be a ruler over your own thoughts and govern them well, so that you may not sway east or west. Be a ruler over your senses and what you look at and what you hear. Be a ruler over the desires of your heart and control them. If you can become a ruler over your self and control it, then you are the person who is fit to be a leader. If you, however, were unable to rule over yourself, nor your tongue, nor your thinking, nor your heart from the inside, then how would you be fit to rule over others? If you were not faithful in what is least, you cannot be faithful over what is much.

One of the monks came to St. Timothy and said to him, "My father, I see that my thoughts are with God always," and so he answered him, "My son, what is better than this is to see your thoughts below all creation."[239]

---

238 *The Letters of John of Dalyatha*, Hansbury M.T., trans. (Piscataway, NJ: Gorgias Press, 2006), 42.
239 Cf. *Give Me a Word: The Alphabetical Sayings of the Desert Fathers*, Wortley J., trans. (Yonkers, NY: SVS Press, 2014), Sisoes 13.

Stay away from positions of authority and first places. Respect all and treat all politely, for what love these do have who treat those below them with respect and reverence. You are capable of respecting the person who is greater than you, but there is no merit for you in this matter, because you are compelled and obliged to respect them. However, the one who respects those below him is humble; he, who respects those who are less than him in rank, knowledge, age, or stature, who preserves their rights and acknowledges their personality, is the person who deserves praise from all. Your honor is not in people submitting to you by virtue of the law or respect, but it is a feeling of reverence that springs from the heart, not just from outward appearances.

3. Self-Contempt and Humility

The person who stays away from the love of praise and honor disdains themselves, for they do not allow anyone to praise them, nor do they allow their own self to praise them either. If one is praised by his self, he must remember his sins and say with the saints:

"I am still walking on the path and have not yet reached the end. Who knows if I will stray along the path? 'Let him who thinks he stands take heed lest he fall.'[240] I have not yet arrived."

---

240 1 Corinthians 10:12.

Part Two: On the Love of Praise

Look to the levels above you. If you look to those who are less than you, you will become prideful and haughty. Why were God's children humble? Because they knew the perfection required of them. They reached high degrees of asceticism, fasting, prayer, self-contempt, and of everything, but before themselves they were weak and wretched, because they knew that there were much higher degrees than [what they had attained in] their lives.

If your soul praises you, say to yourself, "What did I do for my soul to praise me?" Is it for your fasts, prayers, and observance of the commandments that your soul praises you? If your prayer is ordinary, others pray using the psalms. If you pray using some psalms, some pray using all the psalms. If you pray for an hour or more, some stay up the entire night praying. Even if you pray the entire night, some spend day and night in unceasing prayer. What degree have you reached in prayer? Abba Arsenius used to stand in prayer at sunset while looking to the east with the sun behind him, and remain standing in prayer until the sun appeared in front of him. Have you done like him? Abba Macarius of Alexandria trained himself to crucify his mind for several days, such that it was impossible for anything to go through his mind or his thinking besides God. To what extent have you reached? There were fathers who spent many days fasting for weeks [without interruption]. So what have you done?

What degree of charity have you reached? Do you pay tithes? What are tithes, but a Jewish principle, not a Christian one? God ordered the Jews to pay tithes, but to the Christians He said, "Sell all that you have and distribute to the poor."[241] So, have you sold all you have? The Scripture says, "Sell what you have and give alms."[242] Have you done so? And if you truly have sold all that you have, there is an even greater degree: one of the saints was extremely merciful, so he sold all that he had and gave it to the poor. When he did not find anything else to give, he sold himself as a slave and gave the price of his freedom to the poor.

Compare yourself to these levels, and so disdain yourself and humble yourself from within. If you look at those who are less than you, you will be puffed up. An example is a student who passes with a score of 50%. If he compares himself to those who have failed, he will be puffed up because he has passed. However, if he compares himself to those who have passed with higher scores, he will grow smaller in his own eyes. Likewise, you should compare yourself to the higher level so that you may feel that you are still weak and poor and have not done anything yet.

Also, know yourself, that you are dust and ashes, and that you are prone to falling. Try to deny yourself and hide your virtues, and thus do not accept people's praise nor your self-praise.

It is said that two young monks once entered the refectory of a monastery, and at the time, it was

---

241 Luke 18:22.
242 Luke 12:33.

divided into tables, one for elders and another for young monks. The elders invited one of them, so he sat with them, but the other went to a table for the young monks. After they had left, the one who went to the table of the young monks said to his fellow, "How dare you sit with the elders while you are a youth?" So he answered him, saying, "I preferred this, because if I had sat at the table for the young monks, they would have praised me because I am the most senior, and may have put me before them in everything, and invited me to read the blessing and pray. But when I sat at the elders' table, I felt my weakness, and that I did not deserve to speak, and sat shyly with my head bowed the entire time."[243]

This is the true understanding of self and of the lowest seat: that man should feel within himself that he truly is in the lowest seat. For there is a person who, for the sake of being called humble, may choose the lowest seat, all the while vainglory kills them. If you really desire the lowest seat, place your heart in this seat from within. Feel, in your depths, that you are in the lowest seat, even if they seat you at the first seat, saying to yourself: "All these people are better than me."

If you stand and teach children in Sunday school, regard them as angels who are better than you, and ask God that you may have their simplicity, purity, and honor in God's eyes. There was a teacher in Sunday school who,

---

243 Cf. *Give Me a Word: The Alphabetical Sayings of the Desert Fathers*, Wortley J., trans. (Yonkers, NY: SVS Press, 2014), Peter the Pionite 3.

when he encountered a problem, would ask the children in his class to pray for him in his hardship. He used to say, "I have tried their prayers in the problems of my life, and I have felt that they were powerful and greatly effective, more so than my own prayer."

4. Scorning the Praise of People and Renouncing it

The person who renounces praise renounces all the good that people know about him, for he does not want to be praised by them, because he regards people's praise of him and the honor which they offer him as loss. Rather, he desires that his only honor be from God, reiterating Christ's sayings, "I do not receive honor from men,"[244] and, "O Father, glorify Me together with Yourself, with the glory which I had with You before the world was,"[245] wanting to be glorified by God and not by men. So, brother, what glory did you have with the Father before the world was? Your true glory is that you are God's image and likeness. Your true glory is in the loftiness of your character from within, in the purity of your heart, and in God's perception of you.

As for the glory which you receive from people, it is fake, and may be out of ignorance, for those who praise you do not know who you truly are, since they judge according to appearance. They do not read your

---
244 John 5:41.
245 John 17:5.

Part Two: On the Love of Praise

thoughts, they do not know your feelings, your inner emotions, or your hidden sins.

People's praise does not lead you to the kingdom of God, for God is the searcher of hearts and minds and does not depend, in His judgment, on people's thoughts.

Some people praise for the sake of giving compliments, some for encouragement, some due to their manners, some for their own particular reason, and some for flattery. The poor fellow who loves praise cares about being praised no matter how, and relishes in believing what is said about him, whether it is true or false.

People's praise harms many and leads them astray. For this reason, you should befriend one who rebukes and guides you. But if people praise you, remember your sins and shortcomings, and your troubling confessions, and the ugly sins into which you have fallen throughout your life. At that point, the pain of praise will grow lighter.

The most dangerous type of praise is for you to praise yourself from within, when you think within yourself that you are grand and great and wise and righteous, for this is the pride that is present within. You must realize that you are a weak human being, and that all the power you have—if you are walking in God's path—is due to grace supporting you in your life, and that if grace were to let go of you a little, you would fall into the sins you criticized people for, the sins which you thought you were stronger against and would never fall into them one day.

To Get Rid of Praise

One who wishes to be rid of the love of praise must feel the importance of their eternal future, care about it, and make it the main target in their life. Thus, they do not build their glory on earth, but reject worldly honor, and rather care about the honor which God will grant them when the crown of righteousness is placed upon them, and lay up their goods in heaven. It is for this reason that the righteous rejected all forms of honor.

The one who scorns praise flees from the love of visions and revelations, for many of the fathers who fell due to false visions from the demons fell because of the love of praise and honor, and the desire for visions, miracles, wonders, and divine revelations. The demons are capable of appearing in the form of angels of light, even in the form of Christ Himself. Therefore, those who love God must not care about visions or be deceived by them.

The devil once appeared to a saint and said to him, "'I am Gabriel and I was sent to you,' but he said to him: 'Make sure you were not sent to another [person] for I am not worthy,' and [the devil] immediately became invisible."[246] Therefore, if such visions and revelations appear to you, reject them.

The higher the saints rose in their spiritual lives, the more did [the value of] these visions diminish in

---

[246] *The Anonymous Sayings of the Desert Fathers*, Wortley J., trans. (Cambridge, UK: Cambridge University Press, 2013), N.310.

their eyes. It is narrated that one of the great fathers, mighty in the life of the spirit, was walking along the road, praying, his heart filled with God's glory, and his soul completely clung to Him.[247] While he was praying, he found two angels on his right and left, but he did not allow himself to look at either of them, and continued his prayer as usual, repeating in his mind: "Who shall separate me from the love of Christ? Neither angel nor archangel."[248] For this reason, St. Pachomius and Abba Isaac say, "The person who sees their sins is better than the one who sees angels."[249] Therefore, do not ask to see these visions, but feel that you are unworthy. One time, they asked St. Pachomius and said to him, "Tell us about a good vision you have seen," so he answered them, "One who is a sinner like me is not granted visions, but if you want a good sight to see, look at a meek and humble person, for in them you see God, and do not search for a better sight than this."[250]

The prideful person who is a lover of honor desires to see angels, but the humble person desires to see his sins. Visions will not save your soul on the last day, but your knowledge of your follies and shortcomings is that which leads you to salvation.

---

247 See Ibid., N.714.

248 Cf. Romans 8:35, 38.

249 Cf. *The Ascetical Homilies of Saint Isaac the Syrian.* (Boston, MA: Holy Transfiguration Monastery, 2011), 461; *The Anonymous Sayings of the Desert Fathers*, Wortley J., trans. (Cambridge, UK: Cambridge University Press, 2013), N.332.

250 Cf. *Bustan al-Rohban* [Paradise of the Monks]. (Egypt: The Diocese of Beni Swef, 1976), 311–312.

ON THE EGO & THE LOVE OF PRAISE

To reject praise, you must hide your virtuous works and wisdom from people, and make them appear before God only. If you do good for God's sake and not for man's, what does it matter to you if people see this good or not?

One time, a group of monks came to Abba Zeno in Syria and revealed their sins and shortcomings to him. So he looked at them and said, "The Egyptians conceal the virtues they possess and are always accusing themselves of shortcomings which they do not have."[251]

Another time, a monk of Syrian descent was living in Scetis. He came to St. Macarius and said to him, "I have a question, father. When I was in Syria, I was able to fast a great deal and spend days fasting, but now, in Egypt, I cannot complete the day fasting. Why?" Seeing that the monasteries in Syria were in cities in the midst of people, St. Macarius answered him and said, "You used to spend your days fasting because you dined on vainglory, that is, people's praise of you during the fasting and abstinence from food. But here in the wilderness, no one sees you, and hence you quickly become hungry."[252] Because of this, the saints said that if the virtues are known, they are ruined and end; and because of this, they would hide their virtues, wisdom, and knowledge.

The following story is related about Abba Joseph:

---

[251] *Give Me a Word: The Alphabetical Sayings of the Desert Fathers*, Wortley J., trans. (Yonkers, NY: SVS Press, 2014), Zeno 3.
[252] Cf. ibid., Zeno 8.

Part Two: On the Love of Praise

Some elders once visited Abba Antony and Abba Joseph was with them. The elder mentioned a verse from Scripture, wishing to put them to the test. He began to ask, starting with the least of them, what this verse was about and each one began to speak according to his own ability. But the elder said to each one: "You have not discovered it yet." Last of all he said to Abba Joseph: "You then, what do you say this phrase is about?" "I do not know," he replied—so Abba Antony said: "Because he said: 'I do not know' Abba Joseph has indeed discovered the way."[253]

The person who loves praise desires that no one know the answer, so that he alone may answer. However, love "does not rejoice in iniquity, but rejoices in the truth."[254] If you wish to display your knowledge before people in this way, you build your glory on others' losses and people's ignorance, and this is why the saints said, "If you find yourself among the wise, listen and do not speak, and if they ask you about something, say 'I do not know.'" Constantly strive to show your flaws and to conceal your virtues. If God wishes to reveal them, then may His will be done, but you should not reveal them at all lest you receive your reward from people.

To our Lord be all glory and honor. Amen.

---

253 Ibid., Antony 17.
254 1 Corinthians 13:6.

www.ingramcontent.com/pod-product-compliance
Lightning Source LLC
Chambersburg PA
CBHW032137040426
42449CB00005B/288